ProphetAbility
The Revealing Story of Why Companies Succeed, Fail and Bounce Back

Tony Bodoh and Betsy Westhafer

ISBN-13: 9781983100741

DEDICATION

From Betsy:

To my husband, Paul, who inspires me every day to go out and give everything I am to everything I do, and who has never wavered in his belief in me.

To my amazing children and grandchildren, who give me immeasurable joy and gratitude every single day.

And to my mom and dad, who always encouraged me to try new things and who taught me the value of a well-placed comma.

From Tony:

To my wife, Julie, who has been with me every step of this journey. You've given me the courage to become so much more than I knew was possible.

To my daughters, who I can rely on to roll your eyes at my "dad jokes." You inspire me to transform myself so that I can alter the trajectory of human history for you.

To my clients who trust, challenge and bring out the best in me. You've given me the opportunity to transform millions of lives.

RAVE REVIEWS FOR ProphetAbility

"One of Steve Jobs' principles was to make sure you connect the dots. Tony and Betsy have done a great job in connecting the dots from Ancient Kings to modern day CEOs. One of the major failures of today's CEO is to not want to disrupt the norm. This book is filled with stories, advice, and support for making sure today's CEO understands that sometimes disruption is the key to future success. Great advice for any CEO!"

~Jay Elliot - Best-selling author of "The Steve Jobs Way," and CEO of iMedGo

---

"Tony Bodoh and Betsy Westhafer are the prophets of ProphetAbility. They have distilled, dissected, and decompressed their message of artful listening to explain what is really going on with customer experiences. Their ability to read between the lines of what customers are saying is masterful. More importantly, their insight into our human experience can show and teach any business owner or corporate executive a thing or two with their simple yet powerful message in this customer experience masterpiece."

~David Norris - Founder, David Norris Leadership

"Based on the co-authors' combined decades of solid strategy and implementation experience, this book paints a broader and more complete view of what it takes to run a successful customer-centred business. Through multi-layered analysis of numerous case studies, it provides rich insights into what works, what doesn't and importantly: why. As a central point, it highlights the importance of listening to the unfiltered voice of the customer to truly understand what constitutes customer value and provides guidance on how to gain these insights. Truly one of the best business strategy books I have come across in recent years and a must-read for business leaders."

~David Jacques - Customer Experience Pioneer

"As the executive leader of your company, you must possess the predictive power of a seer's crystal ball. Without accurate foresight, you can't lead your company to where the future money will be. You'll find ProphetAbility jammed packed with proven ways to predict and pave the path to your profitable future. Betsy and Tony bring you innovative ideas, incisive insights, pragmatic action steps, and new stunning concepts to identify where your customers are going so that you can meet them there with products and services that they will gladly pay for. This book deserves a place on every executive's desk to be read, reread, and frequently referred to. Pass up these ideas at your peril."

~Mark S A Smith - Podcaster, Author, Business Growth Strategist

"Betsy and Tony have done outstanding work in establishing why customer focus needs to be embraced by the entire organization. Customer programs frequently fail to live up to expectations as the scope and execution is often not done right. This book is a must-read for all executives who realize that customer-led transformations need a lot of thinking, planning and strong execution."

~Shreesha Ramdas - CEO, Strikedeck

"I have known Betsy and Tony for years, and it always amazes me the new insights they share regarding the key areas of relationship marketing and business growth. Particularly their insight into the difference between Customer Experience vs Human Experience is a distinctive, yet powerful (and prophetic), concept that every CEO must learn and understand. Theirs is a must-read book!"

~Dr. Doug Gulbrandsen - Host of Dr. Doug & Friends Radio on K4HD and iHeart Radio, Marketing and Growth Strategist

---

"I found Betsy and Tony have written a must-have desk reference for all business executives who struggle with the constant changing purchasing behaviors of their customers."

~Jim Carras - Board Chairman, Customer Value Creation International

"As a clinical psychotherapist and mentor whose practice focuses on working with successful entrepreneurs and high achievers, I can assure you that Betsy and Tony have hit the mark with this amazing book. Their focus on the human experience is particularly impactful, because that's where it all starts and stops in the world of business. This book is powerful, and I will be recommending it to all my clients and colleagues."

~Dr. Fern Kazlow – Founder of The No Doubt Zone™, Clinical Psychotherapist, Business Consultant, Mentor

---

"Tony Bodoh has been an amazing resource for our company. This book encapsulates the great value we received from Tony's work. If you want to serve your clients and increase profits, read this book!"

~John Boggs - CEO, LSTW Management, LLC

"As the CEO of a startup, I now have in my hands the crystal ball for how to drive our company into the future. Having Betsy as an advisor and mentor for our company helped us get out of the gate in a big way, and now she shares her advice in this book. Every leader from startup founder to the highest levels of the C-Suite needs to read, learn and execute from this book."

~Nick Ripplinger - CEO, Battle Sight Technologies

"ProphetAbility is one of those rare, thought-provoking business books that make you stop in your tracks to re-evaluate your entire way of thinking about your customers and your relationship with them."

~Vinny Ribas - CEO, IndieConnect

"One of our key considerations when assessing which companies to invest in is how much the CEO understands their market. This includes not just the facts and figures, but how much they understand the buying behaviors of their customers. Tony and Betsy have written a book that enforces the significance of listening to the market in ways that go beyond traditional methods. If you think you might someday need investors, read this book now!"

~Melissa Aldridge – Investment Fund Director, Strategist, Advisor

---

"I am going to require my leaders to read this book. It shares real world / current examples that resonate across today's challenges. Thought provoking!"

~Anthony Royer - President and CEO, Allied Dispatch Solutions

"It is the rare leader that has the courage to ask for answers that may not paint them in the best light. And yet, these tend to be the leaders who succeed. This book is a primer for anyone unsatisfied with just being the boss and who is committed to becoming a successful leader."

~Aaron Young - Chairman, Laughlin Associates, Inc.

"ProphetAbility is the playbook of all playbooks. Betsy and Tony have masterfully balanced the science and art to customer listening, providing actionable insights that yield company growth and profitability. Its tone is distinct, exploring how to discover the unexpected and unintended ways customers are receiving value from your products and services. A must-read!"

~Nicolle Paradise - Speaker, Author

FOREWORD

I've spent my career working with prophets.

A couple of decades ago, in the 20th Century, I founded a brand and business-building agency with the express purpose of working side-by-side with them. I said we'd have a mission to, "Inspire Greatness."

The prophet represented that greatness, concentrated.

I had been a serial entrepreneur and an award winning creative director. I knew that my work, my career and my life would only be as great as the people with whom I got to work. I wanted to work with greatness! I would earn my place doing everything in my power to inspire these leaders.

When I was a kid, living in Edison, New Jersey, visiting Edison's laboratory, seeing the framed patents from my Dad's engineering work crowd the walls of our living room, childhood was a constant Socratic seminar in the ways technology alters the future.

But technologists like my Dad were only minor heroes in my father's stories. The true hero was always the prophet.

Jack Welch was the prophet who built General Electric to the very pinnacle of global public companies and made my Dad's career possible. Even in retirement, Dad's habit of investing in prophets has served him well. Steve Jobs, he explained, combined those rare abilities of understanding what the technology would make possible, appreciating what the consumer would love, and knowing how to lead an organization through the needle's eye and ship at the right time. Jeff Bezos was another of my father's discoveries. My stock accounts have benefited from my father's nose for prophets.

I've tended to think of these leaders as "business artists," and "master change agents," and I chased them throughout my career and as my agency grew. As a result, I've been able to participate in many firsts. The first social network, for example, the first auction website, the first online banking account, the first electronic trading app, the first multi-channel direct technology company, the first no-fee credit card, the first company to deliver from the internet to your door, the first online movie and video entertainment site, the first global meal-kit delivery company, and many more.

Working with founders, growth leaders and turnaround masters is the best education money can't buy. Getting to be on the tight team that orchestrated the dramatic turnaround of Weight Watchers over the past few years has been yet another degree.

You'll read about Weight Watchers in this wonderful book.

My world of building brands and businesses has changed dramatically over the past decade, and no one understands why or what to do about it better than Tony and Betsy.

There was a time, not so long ago, when products were commodities differentiated by their advertising.

Back then, the most important thing that separated Campbell's Soup, for example, from the many soups of lesser market share, was the brand. And the brand was built by the advertising, year in and year out over decades.

That world is over. Many large agencies don't know it yet, but their shareholders do.

Today, customer reviews are ubiquitous. Today, your prospects are connected to your customers through social networks and the global web.

Yesterday, the advertising ruled. Today the experience rules.

As in this and all things, working along-side the prophets has served me well.

They always did, rather than just said, inspiring things.

They always built organizations with purpose and culture.

They always put a winning experience first.

More than twenty years ago, I had already learned from them that word-of-mouth truly was the best form of advertising.

Then, to be truthful, it was the exception, whereas today it is the rule.

Tony and Betsy not only understand the rule, they understand it with a depth and complexity that is unmatched. They have analyzed the data, run the experiments and worked with some of the best.

The stories they tell and the principles they share will help you navigate today's market and business landscape. They may even help you be a business artist, a master change agent – a prophet!

Why am I so optimistic about you?

You bought this book. You're on the right track, which also happens to be a much more interesting and worthwhile track.

Enjoy the ride!

~Mark DiMassimo
Chief, DiMassimo Goldstein

ACKNOWLEDGMENTS

Without the support, encouragement and expertise of the following amazing people, we would not have had the opportunity to share this book with you.

Julie Bodoh and Paul Westhafer, thank you for putting up with our long nights, lengthy phone conversations and middle-of-the-night eureka moments.

Mark DiMassimo, thank you for so graciously agreeing to write the foreword for this book and for guiding us along our journey.

Mark S A Smith, you are a force, and we are grateful that you so graciously shared your expertise, enthusiasm and guidance.

Victoria Ballweg, your artistic talents and willingness to drop everything to help us no matter what time of day or night are so very much appreciated.

Mitch Tomlin, thank you for your never-ending enthusiasm for assisting us with this project, and your willingness to do whatever it takes to help us get it over the finish line.

Kids and grandkids, thanks for understanding that our time to share with you was not as we would have wished for the last few months, and for allowing us to make up for that lost time by smothering you with affection in the coming days, weeks and months.

To the scientists and researchers who have gone before us, we stand on your shoulders, and we thank you for the brilliance you shared with us.

And finally, thanks to the planets that aligned so that we were able to come together with our thoughts and passions in order to find these words to share with you, our treasured reader.

TABLE OF CONTENTS

ProphetAbility

INTRODUCTION

Legend tells us that around 1600 BC a goat herder was grazing his flock on the southwestern slope of Mount Parnassus when he noticed that the goats roaming near a chasm in the rock were playing strangely. When he looked into the chasm to investigate he inhaled fumes that put him in a trance. While in the trance the goat herder gained the power to prophesy. Word spread and others came to the spot so that they, too, could learn of future events.

We're told that the danger of falling into the chasm became too great while visitors were in the trance, so it was decided that only one person, a woman born of high society, should be allowed to sit above the chasm and divine the will of first Gaia, then later, Apollo. This shift brought order and established a power for those who controlled the region around 1400 BC. Traditions took hold. Practices and rituals were created and imbued with meaning. A temple was built on the spot and the chasm hidden in a room in the depths of the temple.

Gifts were given to gain an audience and/or to thank the oracle for her prophecies. If the signs were right, once a month for nine months of the year (Apollo left the area during the winter for three months), the oracle would enter the temple chamber to inhale the sweet vapors of coming from the chasm and fall into a euphoric trance during which she would prophesy. Priests and priestesses would interpret and record her prophecies. It is said that she was never wrong, but that sometimes interpreters would alter the messages.

The religion that grew up around the oracle held influence over Greece and Rome for centuries. The oracle's proclamations were essential to key decisions in the Greek nations from when to plant or go to war, and even if they should found a new colony. The belief in the truth of the oracle's prophecies across the known world deepened with every accurate message. The influence lasted for 2,000 years until the 4th century AD when prophesying was outlawed by the followers of a religion based on the word of another prophet, Jesus Christ.

Prophets have been a key part of nearly every great civilization and their messages have been used to promote peace and new unity, or they have motivated followers to revolt. While we are aware of the many prophets that surrounded the Mediterranean, prophets wielded great influence and impacted the formation of governments worldwide. Somewhere around 1142, the Five Nations Iroquois confederacy was formed when a prophet, The Great Peacemaker, Deganawida, counseled the warring tribes in the Americas to find peace.

What is commonly understood about prophets is that they listen to the gods. They share the message they hear, sometimes to their detriment. In a bit of irony, some historians believe we get the phrase, *"don't shoot the messenger,"* from a passage in Plutarch's *Lives.* Later in life Plutarch served the oracle as a priest at Delphi.

"The first messenger, that gave notice of Lucullus' coming was so far from pleasing Tigranes that he had his head cut off for his pains; and no man dared to bring further information. Without any intelligence at all, Tigranes sat while war was already blazing around him, giving ear only to those who flattered him." (Wikipedia: Shooting the messenger)

History has long forgotten many of the prophets, true or false, who were killed or imprisoned for delivering a message the king or his priests did not like. Of those stories we do have, the punishment was often a brutal death. Fortunately, business prophets don't face this same treatment, but many have lost their jobs or had their careers ruined because the CEO did not like what the prophet predicted, or the C-suite and managers (like priests of old) who had a vested interest in the status quo found a way to filter or kill the message so it never reached the CEO.

This book is not about religion, nations at war or the establishment of colonies. Rather, it is about the need for CEOs to listen so they know when their traditions and culture, their competition and their products or services need to be disrupted. And, this book is about how to listen.

THE OVERTHROW OF A RELIGION
The Bounce Back story of IBM

"You are either green and growing or ripe and rotting."

~Ray Kroc
American businessman, McDonalds Global Franchise

At the ripe old age of 107 years, IBM is often seen as the poster child for the ups and downs of a big brand. Sometimes they are ripe and rotting, while at others, they are as green and growing as a Silicon Valley startup. This is the story of how, roughly a quarter of a century ago, IBM bounced back from apparent doom to resurrect into a company that put the customer at the core of everything it did.

In 1993, a time when IBM was hemorrhaging cash, a man by the name of Louis Gerstner, Jr. was brought in to right the ship. What's interesting is that Gerstner was not an IBMer rising through the ranks but rather a customer who had some big issues with the computer company.

With a long history of corporate leadership success, including an 11-year stint at American Express where he increased membership from 8.6 million to 30.7 million, Gerstner was selected after other high-profile computer industry leaders indicated no interest in the role. Upon his arrival, he replaced the CFO, the HR chief and three key line executives, stating, *"Reorganization to me is shuffling boxes, moving boxes around. Transformation means that you're really fundamentally changing the way the organization thinks, the way it responds, the way it leads. It's a lot more than just playing with boxes."*

Unlike many CEOs in similar roles, Gerstner preferred to focus instead on execution, decisiveness, simplifying the organization for speed and breaking the gridlock. This was seen as an overthrow of the old guard and the existing culture.

In his memoir, *Who Says Elephants Can't Dance?,* Gerstner described the pain of changing a culture that had historically been very inwardly focused. Known as a company with a lifetime employment practice since its very inception, over 100,000 employees were laid off after Gerstner's arrival which reversed the belief that employment security had very little to do with performance.

He chose to overturn these things with an undeniable commitment to the customer after his rocky experience as an IBM customer himself.

Back when Gerstner was at American Express, he experienced a problem that needed the attention of IBM, the provider of the company's mainframes. After getting the runaround, he was informed that IBM would not provide service for the entire data center since they had replaced one mainframe with a competitor's product. It was clear to Gerstner that the company had completely lost touch with the needs and desires of their customers.

Shortly after he took the reigns at IBM, with his customer experiences still fresh in mind, he hosted a two-day internal meeting, which ultimately led to a Customer Forum. At the forum were 175 CIOs from some the largest companies in the US.

What he heard at this forum was astounding. He didn't hear problems with products, nor did they focus on pricing. Rather, what surfaced was a collective anger from the CIOs that IBM had allowed the myth that the mainframe was dead to grow and infiltrate the customer organizations, causing the CIOs to lose credibility while the emergence of the PC was gaining some serious momentum. The customers wanted IBM to have their backs, and they felt betrayed.

Gerstner had a prepared speech to deliver to the CIOs, but chose instead to speak extemporaneously. He told them that he was not a technology guy, but rather a former customer who had a deep understanding and strategic view of information technology and that he would bring that to IBM and its customers.

He then laid out four basic expectations to the CIOs. He said:

1. *"We will redefine IBM and its priorities starting with the customer.*
2. *We will give our laboratories free reign and deliver open, distributed, user-based solutions.*
3. *We will recommit to quality, be easier to work with and reestablish a leadership position in the industry.*
4. *Everything at IBM will begin with listening to the customer and delivering what they expect."*

Prior to this Customer Forum, Gerstner held a meeting with the Corporate Management Board, a group of 50 top executives from IBM. When he met with them, he discussed the good things that IBM had working in its favor, but also hit on the challenges they were facing, most notably *"a loss of customer trust supported by some disturbing ratings on quality."*

With that foundation, Gerstner announced OPERATION: Bear Hug. This initiative required that each of the 50 senior managers visit a minimum of five of their biggest customers during the next 3 months, with the goal of listening to the customers, showing them that IBM cared and that they would implement actions as appropriate. The next phase was that each of their collective 200 direct reports would also execute this same exercise.

So there were 250 senior leaders out in the field talking to a minimum of five customers each; a total of at least 1,250 customers being personally visited by an IBM executive through OPERATION: Bear Hug. Taking this a step further, Gerstner required each executive to send him a 1-2 page written report along with copies to anyone else within the organization who could solve the customer's problem.

"I wanted these meetings to be a major step in reducing the customer perception that dealing with us was difficult. I also made clear that there was no reason to stop at five customers and that extra credit would be rewarded."

This was a huge change in the culture of IBM, building everything from the outside in and having the customer drive everything they did in the company. *"It caused quite a stir when people realized that I really did read every report."*

What Went Right

1. Gerstner realized that they had to intricately link everything they did back to the customer. Without that, there would be no hope of growing the company.
2. He utilized his senior leaders to be his prophets, bringing back the message of the people, and then spent time to truly understand what they were saying and not saying.
3. He talked directly with the CIOs and got unfiltered information to which he could align his strategy.

4. He understood the human experience of business, stating, *"Computers are magnificent tools for the realization of our dreams, but no machine can replace the human spark of spirit, compassion, love, and understanding."*

While this is a solid example of a B2B bounce back, it does not mean that IBM continued to thrive upon Gerstner's exit as CEO. In fact, since Gerstner's tenure, things have continued to be a roller coaster ride for the company, with news in March 2018 that IBM would be laying off potentially thousands of employees. With that, however, is the realization that without Gerstner's focus on the customer some 25 years ago, IBM may not have survived.

THE POWER OF A MOMENT...

In late 2016, I (Betsy) had the good fortune to spend a few days at an event supporting our military, working side-by-side with Tony. Although we had met a couple of times prior at various business events, I had never really had the chance to get to know him.

During a break, while sitting in the commissary at Fort Sam Houston in San Antonio, the day before the 2016 election, Tony and I had lunch together and began a conversation that ultimately led us to writing this book, our first together.

Although some time passed before we connected again, it was that moment of conversation, that moment of finding commonality in our thoughts and in our work, that sparked this journey we're now on of helping organizations understand the impact that the human experience and strategic listening have on growing a business, from the customer to the CEO and everyone in between.

In the pages that follow, you will read stories of success, stories of failure and stories of bounce back. Despite the different conclusions in these stories, the one thing they have in common is that some*_one_*, not some*_thing_*, influenced the ultimate outcomes. Business in and of itself is a human experience, and within it, there are a multitude of individual human experiences that directly impact the results. There is no version of artificial intelligence than can yet replace the power of the human experience.

A CEO is human. Customers are human. Employees are human. Vendors are human. Investors are human (most of the time). Every single decision a business makes is made by a human directly or it is made by a person who ultimately decided on the rules a machine should use to make the decision.

Tony and I spent countless hours on the phone, texting, and sending each other video monologues on our thoughts as we developed this book. One of the things he said very early on really struck me.

"In B2B, we don't do business with other businesses, we do business with people who work in other businesses."

We will dive deeper into the topics of moments, influence, strategic listening, disruption, divergent collaboration, culture and many other areas in which business is impacted by the ability to more deeply understand the role that the human plays. We will illustrate our points by giving you real life examples, the good, the bad and the ugly. You will see that at the root of all things, human experience in business is the ability to really listen deeply for what the humans associated with your business are seeking at a level they may not even be aware of, and how to make those insights the foundation for everything you do moving forward. You will emerge with a deeper appreciation for the mindset of a prophet - *"a person regarded as an inspired teacher or leader; a person who foretells or predicts what is yet to come."*

Our objective is to provide you with deep insights that will change your perspective on how to lead your business. Our infinite hope is that your experience in reading this book will be a transformational moment for you.

THE ROLES OF THE GODS, KINGS, PRIESTS AND PROPHETS

No matter the culture—Christian, Greek, Roman, Egyptian, Business—the roles played by gods, kings, priests, and prophets have a definitive thread of commonality. By exploring the roles of each and the relationships between them, we can gain a better understanding of why organizations succeed, fail or bounce back.

The Role of the Gods

HISTORICAL PERSPECTIVE
The gods are the ones who must be pleased, for the true power lies with them. The goal is to be in agreement with what the gods think and want, and it is up to the powers that be to listen to and hear what the gods are prescribing. To do otherwise is almost certain death for the kingdom.

BUSINESS TRANSLATION
The customers are the ones who must be pleased, for they are the ultimate decision makers on the purchase. The goal is to be in alignment with the market, and it's up to the CEO to determine how to position the company based on where the market is heading. To do otherwise is almost certain failure for the company.

The Role of the King

HISTORICAL PERSPECTIVE
The role of the king is to govern the kingdom. The future of the kingdom lies within the hands of the king, and as such, the king must be focused beyond today or tomorrow. Think back to the time of droughts and famines. The king needed to think three, five, even seven years out to have a plan for protecting his subjects and the kingdom itself. It's the role of the king to ensure that not only will the kingdom survive, but that it will thrive well into the future.

The interesting thing that happens in kingdoms of all cultures is that there can be a battle between the priests and the prophets who serve at the pleasure of the king. The battle is one of influence. Who among them will influence the king and the direction he takes?

BUSINESS TRANSLATION:
The role of the CEO is to create and execute the vision for the company. The future of the organization lies with the CEO, and as such, the CEO must be looking beyond the monthly, quarterly or even annual reports. Think back to companies that allowed their short-term thinking to destroy the future of the business. The CEO needs to think three to five years into the future in order to protect the employees and the organization itself. It's the CEO who gets paid to ensure that the company not only survives but also thrives well into the future.

The interesting thing that happens in companies in all industries is that there can be a battle between members of the C-Suite. The battle is one of influence. Who among the C-Suite members will influence the CEO and the direction he takes?

The Role of the Priests

HISTORICAL PERSPECTIVE

The rule of order is the function of the priest. His job is to sanctify, purify, and be the holder of the rituals and traditions that support the law of the land. This leader religiously has his eye on governance, processes, and is the keeper of the true history of the land. The question that never escapes the priest is, *"How do we bring order to what would otherwise be chaos?"* Without this structure, a society cannot effectively be sustained. Priests use religion to maintain this order. The priest can often control what the king cannot, but also has a desire to be an influencer to the king. Sometimes the priest succeeds in influencing the king and sometimes he fails. If he fails, he may be eliminated if the king has a contrary vision, or the king may adopt a pagan religion and get rid of all the priests under his reign.

BUSINESS TRANSLATION

Where the king and the CEO can be compared directly, the priest has no direct comparable title in business. Anyone who has the mindset and behaves in a way to preserve the rituals, traditions and rules of the company is playing the role of a priest. They want stability, status quo and certainty. They oppose disruption, chaos, and often, even innovation.

There is a need for priests in companies. An efficient company requires systems, policies, processes and procedures. Data and information must be cleansed and recorded with one version of the truth so all teams can communicate effectively with each other. And, the priests are essential to influence the king to say "no" to the large number of things that would take the business away from its mission.

The Role of the Prophet

HISTORICAL PERSPECTIVE
The prophet can hear the gods and it's his role to be the messenger to the king. But it's critical to remember that there are real prophets and false prophets.

The prophet spreads a message of the promise of the gods, or the wrath of the gods, or how to be faithful and loyal to the gods. The prophet is sent by the gods to bring society back into alignment with their wishes. But sometimes the messenger (the prophet) is beheaded for the message that they deliver, either because the king doesn't like it or the people rebel. Conversely, sometimes the prophet is accepted and praised. The prophet can help a king avert the destruction of his kingdom.

BUSINESS TRANSLATION

Like the priests, prophets in business have no specific title. Again, being a prophet is more about mindset and behaviors. Naturally, you may be able to find a concentration of prophets in particular departments or teams, but that is a matter of mindset, not role.

The prophet in a business serves the role of challenging the status quo, traditions and customs that no longer add value for the customer and therefore for the shareholders. The prophet keeps a foot in the present, listening to the challenges of the customers, but more importantly, the prophet listens to what they are inspired by, what causes them to feel admiration, awe and gratitude toward the company. Then, the prophet must see into the future to understand how the company can use this insight. Finally, he must construct a story that influences the king to decide on a new direction.

Prophets in business need to listen using sound research practices, and they must understand human experience and human desires if they are to be successful in their ability to see the future and influence the future of the company. There are many dangers for prophets. Priests will oppose them and the king may ignore them. But, they must courageously persist.

Business in Today's Times

Throughout the following pages, you will see examples of how modern-day players in these roles have interacted, and how their organizations have succeeded, failed, or bounced back as a result. We will dive into the theories and psychology behind these organizational dynamics and provide you with some high-level strategies for ensuring that your company is ultimately ProphetAble™.

CHAPTER 1
WHAT'S OLD IS NOW

OVERVIEW AND CHALLENGES

It's no secret that the times, they are a-changin'...fast.

Historically, we have seen massive transformation just within our lifetimes that is nothing short of awe-inspiring. These changes, whether technological or economic, psychological or social, create a new world not only for customers, but also for C-suite executives. Given that the CEO is responsible for the vision and culture of the company, they have to create a future vision that includes their team, technology, and customers. These are indeed challenges with no existing roadmap.

> *"A CEO creates a future that does not yet exist using methods that have not yet been invented."*
>
> ~Mark S A Smith
> author, podcaster, entrepreneur

Let's break it down.

Transformation through Technology

Since the introduction of the iPhone in 2007, we have completely changed the way we communicate and the way others communicate with us. Equipped with ubiquitous access to data streams and virtually unlimited data download capability, we have, at our fingertips, quantities and qualities of data that were not previously available to royalty. We access all of human history, invention, and wisdom through our mobile devices.

As people use their mobile devices every waking moment for just about every human function, we now have the ability to view, track, and analyze a massive amount and variety of data, with additional advances coming so fast and furious that it will soon exponentially increase the amount of available data—to a level almost hard to even fathom. Think the evolution to 5G (gigabit to your device), artificial intelligence, augmented reality, and virtual reality. Within a few years of this book, there will be new, more advanced technology available.

Where we have advanced since 2007 when the iPhone was introduced is phenomenal. As business leaders, the access we now have to data allows us to gain a more comprehensive understanding of customer behavior than ever before. People not only use these tech devices, including iPads, tablets and the like to live their lives, but businesses are now being run by executives from a device that is literally attached to their hips.

So with that historical perspective, what can we expect in the next decade? Research in *Rethinking Transportation 2020-2030: The Disruption of Transportation and the Collapse of the Internal-Combustion Vehicle and Oil Industries* predicts, for example, that by 2030, 95 percent of the road miles in the United States will be driven by electric, self-driving cars which will be managed via corporate-owned fleets. By 2021 buying a new car will cost four to ten times more than using available automated transportation services. The trend is moving so fast in this direction that while editing this book, Waymo (an independent self-driving technology company and Google spinoff) ordered 62,000 Chrysler Pacifica Hybrid Minivans. In theory, individuals will no longer own cars. Imagine the disruption to various industries, beyond just the automotive industry, when this happens. Here are just a few questions that come to mind:

- What happens to the auto insurance industry?
- How many and what type of mechanics will we need?
- Will auto dealerships disappear?
- If we don't need garages to store our cars, will we need garage doors, a $4B industry?
- Will we need parking lots in cities? What about asphalt companies?
- How will the construction industry be impacted as the need for parking garages decreases and lots become available for more high rises?
- Will municipalities lose significant revenue due to the reduction in moving violations?
- Will we need traffic lights? If not, how much power will that save?
- With no DUIs, what will be the impact on the court system when a massive income stream disappears?

Tech disruption is our new normal, and no industry can claim immunity. This leads us into the economic impact resulting from these technological revolutions.

Economic Transformation

Executives with still-healing scars from the economic meltdown circa 2008, avoid capital expense lock-in, which hobble flexibility in uncertain markets. This demands new, transformational approaches to business infrastructure and manufacturing strategies. The result: cloud IT everywhere, and most companies completely outsource manufacturing.

You or probably someone you know has lost their house, cars, marriage, business, and their minds riding out the last economic disaster. Those of us left standing won't make that same mistake again.

- Due to losses in the stock market, boomers were forced to work longer than planned or re-enter the workforce after retirement.
- The Gen Xers were not being promoted as would be expected, meaning they weren't spending money at an accelerated rate and they, too, lost money in the market.
- About 1 in 3 of all 18-24 year olds polled by census.gov rely on their parents for financial assistance.
- Millennials are coming out of college with enormous amounts of debt, but without the promise of high-paying jobs from which to repay their loans. They aren't buying homes, cars, and other traditional big-ticket items historically associated with their age ranges.
- According to the Allianz Generations Apart Study an overwhelming 93% of post-crash skeptics - which includes a cross-section of Gen Xers and boomers who experienced six or more effects of the crash - said that the 2008 crash still haunts them. Accordingly, more than 9 in 10 (93%) believe that the traditional definition of retirement is now a "romantic fantasy of the past."

As a result of the non-discriminating financial impacts listed above, we are seeing a shift in the underlying assumptions of the economy.

Business Transformation

Now, as we move forward, present day has us creating an entirely new economic machine, including the rise of unregulated platforms such as cryptocurrency, a monetary exchange that is writing its own rules while philosophically standing against any form of governmental interference. Companies are now creating their own forms of currency while crypto exchanges, similar to stock exchanges, are simultaneously being established, giving investors more options toward which they can direct their funds.

The very nature of how we are going to create currency, exchange currency and establish value for goods and services is radically shifting. Proof that the crypto form of value exchange is not just a flash-in-the-pan radical idea meant for people who are inclined to buy lottery tickets is the fact that institutional investors, including JP Morgan Chase, Goldman Sachs, and Bank of America are now participating in an arena that could directly threaten the very existence of their own industry.

These technological and economic shifts drive more than just theories and evolution. They have a very definite impact on how people live, work and play which results in societal shifts that leave some longing for the good old days.

Social Transformation

Depending upon your perspective, the pace and impact of disruption is either exhilarating or scary as hell, or for some, a little of both. Consider these points regarding the social changes exhibited between the boomer and millennial generations:

- 1 in 3, or about 24 million 18- to 24-year-olds lived in their parents' home in 2015
- The millennial views on the environment, materialism and social responsibility are what define them as a generation and are radically different from the 80's, known as "The Decade of Excess," and the "Me Generation," which gave us McMansions, 3-car garages and self-indulging preppies.
- According to Goldman Sachs, "Millennials have been reluctant to buy items such as cars, music and luxury goods. Instead, they're turning to a new set of services

that provide access to products without the burdens of ownership, giving rise to what's being called a 'sharing economy.'"

What's even more fascinating is that the post-millennial generation, the Gen Z's, who were born between 1995 and 2012, are making their mark on the market and corporate America even at their tender ages. For example, Reuters reported in November 2017 that Nestle set a goal to source only eggs from cage-free hens for all its food products globally by 2020. It's fair to assume that this decision is a direct response to the shifting views of their younger customer base who are moving away from dairy products and who are committed to the ethical treatment of animals.

"Our purpose is to enhance quality of life and contribute to a healthier future. This includes ensuring decent welfare standards for animals that are reared for the ingredients used in our products."

~Nestle

It's worth noting that in five to ten years, these Gen Z's will not just be influencing the purchasing behaviors of their parents, but will have their own money to spend on goods and services that fit with their socio-economic beliefs. This significantly impacts companies and the way they must move forward.

As you can see, the gap between the boomer generation and the Gen Z's is significant and has implications far and wide, particularly as it relates to their consumer behaviors.

Why Does This Matter to a CEO?

Having a deep understanding of the historical shifts between generations as it relates to technology, economics and social norms is important for CEOs for this reason: It is the CEO whose job it is to look beyond the month-end, beyond the quarterly reports, beyond the annual meeting of shareholders. It's the CEO who is thinking about what happens three to five years from now.

Others in the C-Suite are thinking toward the future as well, but not as far out as the CEO. For example, the CMO may be thinking about marketing technology that will be required and how they will need to market in the next couple of years. The Chief Product Officer may be thinking about the product roadmap for the next 12-24 months. The Chief Sales Officer has his or her sights set on making their monthly numbers. The time horizons for the various leaders vary widely depending upon their roles.

"The main thing that has caused companies to fail, in my view, is that they missed the future."

~Larry Page
computer scientist, co-founder of Google

It's the CEOs, for the most part, who are thinking about the future three to five years from now and they better get it right, because their team, customers and investors count on them. They are thinking about how to address current 14-year-olds when they are in college and beyond. The reality is, no one else in the organization is really paid to think at that level, and no one else can.

When a CEO looks to their CMO, CIO, CPO (R2D2 has C3PO) for insight, they get a 0-2 year perspective based on the individual executives' key performance indicators (KPIs). That is simply not enough to successfully move forward. Rather, B2B and B2B2C CEOs would be well served to have deep dive conversations with the CEOs of their key customers. Why? Because those CEOs also have a charge to be thinking three to five years into the future. They are also exploring how technology, economics and social changes are impacting their businesses. And, they also need to be talking to their fellow CEOs to ensure that they have relevant and accurate insights to lead their companies into the future. Imagine the impact of having those conversations side-by-side with CEO peers from your key customers.

One of Betsy's Customer Advisory Board clients often repeats this mantra that drives their unwavering commitment to engaging customers in an effort to foresee the future: *"We just don't know what we don't know."* Being mindful and open to uncertainty, and putting processes around how to address it is a strength exhibited by forward-thinking, strong executive leaders.

The best GPS can't give directions until it knows where you are and where you want to go. CEOs are the GPS of the company so must have topsight (where the organization is) and foresight (where the organization needs to go).

However, that's not to say that CEOs should not also be focused on the unfiltered information that comes out of the customer base today. In fact, it's important that the CEO is in touch with today, with next quarter, with five years from now. They need insights from the entire spectrum. The challenge, however, is that the transaction-oriented customer feedback cannot be strategic. For example, employees who manage incoming user-level customer feedback turn it over to the help desk to solve, a reactive approach. To be fair, in some

21

companies you also have your Customer Success Managers (CSMs) proactively solving problems and educating clients to keep them out in front of potential issues. They are moving from reactive to proactive, which of course, is a very good thing. The time horizon is moving out a bit, but it remains a transactional approach rather than a strategic one.

Therein lies the gap. When the organization is listening at the transactional level, they probably aren't interpreting for the strategic level. What gets pushed up to the CEO and to the other members of the C-suite are scores and metrics (CSAT, NPS, Ease of Use, etc.) which indicates *what* is happening but does not tell *why* it happened or *how* to fix it. It's a symptom, not a diagnosis. The market dominance challenge lies within that gap.

To close this gap, transactional feedback must be put into the context of the life of the customer. This feedback becomes strategic when the company takes a longer-term perspective and asks a new set of questions:

- Who does our customer want to become?
- What do they want to accomplish?
- What is meaningful to them?
- What identity do they wish to reinforce?
- Which identity do they wish to change?
- Which relationships are they trying to deepen?
- What do they do to reach their optimal performance?
- What do they want to feel?

For each of these questions the company must ask,

- "Why is that?" "Why is that important to you?" "Why is that important to me?"
- "How are they already trying to do these things?"
- "What impedes their transformation?

Case Study – Xtracycle

A few years ago Tony worked with Xtracycle. The CEO, Ross Evans, invented a version of his cargo bike over 20 years ago while doing charitable work in Latin America. He saw that farmers had a hard time getting their crops to market because the roads were not suited to pull-behind wagons or carts. So, he went to work welding together an old bike frame with an extension that allowed the farmer to carry a few hundred pounds of produce on the back of his bicycle. Over time, Ross perfected the design and started a company making and marketing his longtail cargo bike, the Edgerunner, as a replacement for cars in cities.

When Ross contacted us, he was trying to adapt to a changing market. *"The biggest issue here was coming from competition. Many new businesses were entering the cargo bike market and even though they had inferior product and no brand or story, they were growing much more than we were absorbing any growth in our market. That said, ultimately we found that we had to shift our channel strategy and add a high-touch B2C delivery mechanism in order to meet demand and gain negotiation leverage with dealers."*

Ross wanted to know where he should focus his attention and his resources. The first thing we studied was how they were already capturing stories from customers and we recommended that they add specific questions to their bike registration process to collect richer information immediately after delivery of the customer's Edgerunner. Then we examined the customer feedback they collected through their online reviews, surveys and customer support. We analyzed these stories, not from a transactional perspective, but from a strategic perspective. How should Xtracycle be positioned?

We asked the questions outlined above: Who do Xtracyclers (they are a loyal and friendly group) see themselves becoming? What do they want to accomplish? What is meaningful to them? In the end, we were able to understand not only the customer, but also the human who claimed the identity of being an Xtracycler. As a result, Ross and his team have been able to create an online B2C experience that is miles ahead of the competition while still supporting his B2B2C model.

Dangers of AI and Big Data

One of the dangers of analyzing transactional customer feedback is that people are hoping for and relying on artificial intelligence and big data to tell them what they should do. And while these tools are more advanced than we have ever had before and can reveal patterns and nuances, they still are only revealing the "what" rather than "why."

A simple version of the big data/AI logic goes like this: We know that if a segment of customers has done "A," "B" and "C" in a particular time frame, they tend to do "D" next. So then a company may say, *"Let's make this specific offer."* It is more complex than this series of if/then statements, which means it can be powerful, particularly as it relates to product development and roadmaps. But without understanding the "why," which comes down to the psychology of the person, and without understanding what they are actually saying, companies run into challenges. AI can only tease out patterns and trajectories. It doesn't do well without tens to hundreds of thousands of "experiences" before it can reliably recognize the patterns within the consumer chaos.

"Results are obtained by exploiting opportunities, not by solving problems."

~ Peter F. Drucker
management consultant, educator, author

For example, a CEO may say, *"Here's the gap I see. I've got lower level, transactional programs happening (Customer Service, Customer Success) and most of what is getting pushed up to the to me are the metrics. We've got X percent satisfaction scores, we've got Y percent of retention (or renewals), but we still don't know why people are leaving. Let's really understand what people are telling us, or more importantly, NOT telling us. What are the leading indicators? We need to track the language and the conversations that are happening. We need the human factors behind all these scores."*

"Think like a customer and communicate like a CFO."

~Nicolle Paradise,
speaker, author

International Speaker, Head of Experience at TEDx San Francisco, and "Top 25 Global Influencer," Nicolle Paradise, often speaks of the need to not just understand the numbers, but rather operationalize the why behind the numbers.

"Nearly all B2B organizations are fluent in calculating metrics for why customers might leave, yet often lack the metrics for asking—then measuring and operationalizing—why customers would stay. The opportunity for radical growth then is to 'think like a customer and communicate like a CFO.' Partner directly with your customers to re-examine the friction points that led them to your product, then understand how they are measuring impact internally. Subtract the monthly or annual contract value from that measured impact and it will yield the customer ROI. This matures the conversation beyond advocacy and delight; it communicates that your company is contributing to the growth of your customers and demonstrates, financially, why they stay."

Customers Tell You Where They Intend to Go... Until They Change Their Mind

We've worked closely with clients in a variety of industries (B2B, B2B2C and B2C) and found that when we analyze the patterns of the language in customer feedback from a few weeks to as many as six months before an event, that language is actually highly predictive of the eventual customer decision. Here are a few examples:

- We showed an insurance company which customers had a greater likelihood of canceling their account months before it happened.
- We discovered how to predict which small business owners and executives would be likely to buy one of three training programs, and which was the right offer to make.
- We showed a training company how they could use educational marketing content weeks before an offer was made to move small business owners from the mindset of a non-buyer to the mindset of a buyer who would successfully use the program to grow their companies.

This tracking of language and conversation, whether done in person or by artificial intelligence, is only going to get more difficult. Right now we can track language through emails, surveys and other text-based methods, but as we move into a more visual/video world, that data becomes much harder to mine. Instead of mining text, we will have to mine video. We will have to mine voice intonations, pupil dilation, facial emotion expressions in addition to the speech and text. We may even measure other forms of biofeedback like some gaming systems do today in real time; then consider what happens when augmented and virtual reality are mainstream like smartphones are today. After all this analysis, we have to synthesize these separate data streams into a single coherent stream to draw the correct conclusion.

Because we are still on the edge of that technology, it becomes a very pricey proposition. It's just not commercially viable yet and won't be feasible for most companies in the near term. With that being the case, we have to dive into the data and tools we do have in order to bridge the gap. The way to do that is to gather more qualitative data that can be synchronized with your quantitative data and share the insights with the senior level in a structured and meaningful way without filtering it.

Summary:
CEOs can't rely on their staff, who have shorter operating time frames, for future vision.

Ask yourself...
- How can I better work with my customers (B2C) and customer executives (B2B and B2B2C) to co-create the future?
- What do I need to feed my crystal ball, giving me a clearer view of the future?

Ask your Executive Team...
- How far in the future do you plan?
- What would you need to occasionally look one more year further?

Your Action Plan
- Actively seek others who are futurists and business leaders to routinely hold forward-looking conversations.
- Keep a journal of your future visions, even when you have no idea how to accomplish them.
- Operationalize how you listen to your customers.

THE LAND WITHOUT A PROPHET
The Failure Story of Toys R Us

The journey to the graveyard for Toys R Us was long and slow, beginning back in 2005 when they were the target of a leveraged buyout. That was the beginning of the end, and the company was put on life support in September 2017 when they filed for bankruptcy protection just prior to the holiday season. However, for multiple reasons, the attempt failed and the toy store was nearly six feet under by early 2018.

This is a story of signs that were missed and a lack of a strong prophet who challenged the culture and status quo of the company.

Upon the announcement of the closing of all 182 Toys R Us stores in the US, the blame game commenced. The company blamed Walmart, Target and Amazon for deeply discounting their toys and selling them as loss leaders, making up their profitability in other areas, a strategy not available to an exclusive toy seller like Toys R Us. However, that simple explanation for their failure is but one of many.

Let's go back again to 2005, when a leveraged buyout of Toys R Us was orchestrated by Bain Capital and KKR. These two private equity firms invested a small amount of capital, and then borrowed money based on the assets of Toys R Us, including the real estate, buildings, brand name, etc. Their goal was to invest a minimal amount of money, maximize the debt on the books and allow for a scenario where Toys R Us could pay the interest on the debt while the private equity firms extracted as much capital as possible out of the company. This was a very short-term strategy that ultimately failed due to the following reasons:

1. They assumed that the value of retail, including the value of the real estate, would continue to rise which did not happen. In fact, just the opposite occurred

when the brick and mortar retail world began taking a downward turn.

2. They misjudged how aggressively Walmart, Target and other big box stores would attack by offering toys as loss leaders for the indefinite future.

3. They completely misjudged the impact of Amazon. Even though the online giant had been around for eight years at this point, they really didn't understand online retail to be a serious threat to their business.

As the retail economy shifted from brick and mortar to online, it dramatically worked against them in many ways, most notably with regard to the buyout. The value of their assets plummeted, they lost the ability to borrow against those assets, and the collateral serving against those assets dried up. Financially speaking, the financiers had a very short-term vision, extracting as much cash out as fast as possible—essentially using the debt structure as an ATM to get their money back out while other stakeholders suffered losses in the long term.

But again, the blame does not just rest here. The CEO failed to see that this vision was short-sighted nor was he prepared for the changes in the market.

When they filed for bankruptcy protection, a move designed to appease vendors who needed assurances that they would get paid, they also showed their hand at their instability, causing customers to question the toy store's ability to make returns or honor purchased gift cards. This obviously had a negative impact on their holiday season sales. And finally, again by showing their hand, they opened the door for the likes of Walmart, Amazon and Target to land the final blow.

No Prophet, No Vision

Toys R Us did not have the foresight to see the devastating implications of filing bankruptcy just prior to the holiday season. This includes the impact on sales and the reaction of the three giants who were competing against them.

Their lack of vision is also exemplified by not identifying the shift in consumer behavior as customers moved to an online preference. The leaders of Toys R Us made the assumption that people would just keep coming into the store as they had historically done. Not only did they not lead with a three to five year vision, they didn't even recognize the patterns that were emerging in the here and now.

The question arises: Did the CEO not listen to his prophets (the messengers of the people) or did he just not have any? Same result either way.

ECONOMIC DISRUPTION: THE NEW NORMAL

When exploring organizational transformation, it's critical to have a deep understanding of economic transformation and the role disruption plays in it.

Let's begin with a B2C example that, if you are a lover of a good cup of joe, will be certain to resonate.

In a book written in 1999 by Joseph Pine II and James Gilmore, they illustrated the principles of the Experience Economy. They proposed that the economy had gone through several evolutions from the Commodity Economy to the Product Economy to the Service Economy to the Experience Economy. They demonstrated this evolution (as have others who have written about it) with a variety of examples. One of the favorite examples to use is that of the coffee industry.

The economy has evolved from a Commodity Economy, where at the ground level, as a commodity producer you could earn roughly $.05 per cup for growing the coffee beans. When you turn coffee into a product, like Maxwell House, putting branding, marketing, and shelf placement around it, you make about $0.15 per cup. If you have a diner or a convenience store or in some way you actually make the coffee so it's easy for someone to just grab a cup and run or drink a cup with their meal, then you are looking to make about $1.50 per cup. But, if you create an experience, as is the case with Starbucks, known as "The Third Place" (work, home, Starbucks) you provide more than the coffee. You provide a place where people can gather, network, chill, run their business and at that point, you have people willing to pay between $3.00 and $5.00 for a cup of coffee.

Pine and Gilmore go on to explain that at the Commodity level, we are **extracting** value. At the Product level, we are **making** value. At the Service level, we are **delivering** value, and at the Experience level, we are **staging** value. They conclude by defining the Experience Economy as *"selling consumers events that stimulate the senses and emotions to create memories."*

Starbucks is trying to sell you on an event. Going into their store, remembering what it's like to have a great conversation with someone, over the smell of freshly brewed coffee. That's what they stimulate so that when you feel the need for a coffee or a great conversation, you think of Starbucks.

So how does this apply in a B2B world?

In the world of hospitality, you've got hotels winning big contracts with large companies by giving better rates to their business travelers. There are also billions of dollars a year being spent on the meetings industry, much of which is a B2B play. A company sponsors a conference and there are a number of businesses involved in creating and executing the event. People attend these conferences representing their businesses, which points to that fact that even in B2B, there is a customer experience.

In B2B, we don't do business with other businesses. We do business with people who work in other businesses. As is the case with customers in the B2C world, these people also have human experiences, and that must be considered as much in the B2B space as it is in B2C. In B2B, you must still stimulate the senses and emotions to create memories if you want to succeed in the Experience Economy.

Maslow's Hierarchy and Economic Value

We have been showing companies the link between customer needs, wants and experiences and Maslow's Hierarchy of Needs since at least 2008. During that time we showed that more economic value is created when the higher needs of the customers are being served. In other words, the growth of spending near the top of the pyramid on experiences that satisfy customer needs for belonging, esteem and self-actualization has been growing exponentially.

It was a pleasant surprise when, in the September 2016 issue of Harvard Business Review, a pyramid model containing thirty elements of consumer value was published. Then in March of 2018 HBR.com published an article based on research from Bain that introduced a pyramid model with forty elements of value for B2B buyers. Others finally made a similar connection.

If you take a look at the Personal Development/Human Performance industry, a $9.9B industry as of 2018, the entire industry is based upon the highest levels of Maslow's Hierarchy of Needs. Its core is self-actualization, self-esteem and love and belonging. Companies are generating value and people are buying more and more products there. Interestingly, the same thing holds true in B2B but it's not as clear to see. For example, we have people hiring coaches so that they can become better sales people. We have leaders hiring consultants to teach them how to run their businesses better. We have training companies like Franklin Covey offering B2B training with a focus on how to execute. There is an abundance of content marketing out there that teaches business people how to grow, how to become unique in their chosen fields and ultimately how to become better at what they do. So as you can see, there is a shift happening even in B2B.

We have to educate. According to The 2016 Content Preferences Survey Report, 79 percent of B2B buyers consume three or more pieces of content before reaching out to a sales person. They are educating themselves and moving up on Maslow's Hierarchy of Needs beyond the lower levels to the higher levels so that they can be aware before they even reach out to a sales representative.

Moving Beyond the Experience Economy

In their work, Pine and Gilmore actually predicted the next evolution, that of the Transformation Economy. The next level beyond staging value is *guiding* value. Specifically, a company that sells transformation is literally selling the buyer on *"a series of experiences that guide them through learning, taking action and eventually achieving their aspirations and goals."*

Think about how different that is compared to the Experience Economy. The Experience Economy is about creating a memory through a particular event. But the Transformation Economy is about a whole series of events that really transform the individual into someone different, helping them to achieve what they aspire to achieve in their life.

A simple example of this is the Tony Robbins organization, the producer of personal growth weekend events. Or, think of a user conference for your favorite software company where customers are coming in to learn, grow and better understand how to extract value from their purchase. These are transformations.

But we can go even deeper into this principle. For example, one of Tony's (Bodoh not Robbins) clients sells software to the federal government. Through the discovery process, Tony's team identified that a particular leader wanted to leave a legacy and to impact the agency in a way that would ensure its long-term success. His retirement was within reach, so this desire had a level of urgency to it.

For this leader, his focus was on the self-esteem and self-actualization that results from being recognized and seen as someone who was able to achieve something significant. So in crafting the sales message to this person, the focus became not just about features and functions of the software, but rather, how those features and functions will contribute to the legacy he hoped to leave. This is a definite shift in mindset. Rather than focusing only on the features and benefits, which by the way are still very important, the conversation was centered on the transformation that would occur within the agency as a result of purchasing this product. It was selling the legacy by providing a product that would deliver it. There is real magic in helping the purchaser see how your product or service helps them transform into the person they seek to be.

Strikedeck CEO, Shreesha Ramdas, notes that many people are of the belief that you can make customers successful just by focusing on creating successful outcomes. So in other words, can you get your product to create successful business outcomes for your customers? If so, you are making your customers successful.

"I agree with that," says Shreesha, *"but I say you should go beyond that. It's not just about creating successful business outcomes, it's also about making your sponsor successful in presenting a strong business case to the organization. When you can tie your sponsor getting a promotion or*

a reward directly to your product, that's when you know you've made your customer successful."

Shreesha adds, *"We have a customer that is a public company in New York. I felt on top of the world when John called me and said, 'We got the innovation award this quarter because of our Strikedeck implementation.'"*

"You should always work hard to make the organization successful, but you should also make sure that you are also working on behalf of your key sponsor and the folks who have invested their faith in your product or service."

~Shreesha Ramdas
CEO, serial entrepreneur

But there are some inherent challenges with this in the B2B world that you don't necessarily have in B2C due to the complexity of the organizational structure. Because there may be multiple decision makers in a B2B sale (User, Purchaser, IT department head, CFO, CEO), you have to address the needs of each individual and how they want to be guided through the sales experience. According to LinkedIn's *"Definitive Guide to Selling to Multiple DecisionMakers,"* there is an average of 6.8 people involved in each B2B purchase decision.

This is especially common for software companies. Tech companies go through a Requirements Gathering Phase in which they identify what they want to accomplish. Done the old way, they are trying to figure out which features and benefits to create, but done right, they would approach this with a transformation mindset.

The Customer is the Product

In their book, *The Experience Economy,* Pine and Gilmore state that in reality, the customer is the product. Think it about it like this:

Say you take a piece of wood and put it into a factory. There it can become a desk, a chair, a table, a shelf or a multitude of other products. It goes through a number of machines and is transformed into a finished product.

In the Transformation Economy, the person comes to the process in whatever raw material state they may be in. The customer is like the log on the one end of the factory. You, the company, guide them through a series of experiences that morph them, turn them and alter how they see the world. You will change how they see themselves and will transform them into someone amazing, someone they desire to be. So the customer is actually the product. Through the process, they come out on the other end as someone different. This is true in both B2B and B2C.

They are also the buyer, which makes the Transformation Economy much more unique, interesting and exciting than any other economy we've had before.

If you are in the B2B world, you may say, *"I need a software so that I can serve my customers better."* Or, *"I need some help in designing and building our new corporate headquarters."* Or, *"I need to buy some equipment for our factory."* In other words, you have vendors, and those vendors should be considering how they are going to help you and your business transform. They need to know who you and your company want to become as a result of doing business with them.

Fundamentally, the CEO needs to understand, whether B2B or B2C, how their customers want to transform over the next three to five years. Who do they want to become? How do they want to transform?

Experience vs. Transformation

In the Experience Economy, people pay for what they expect to feel. They buy the feeling and the promise of a memory. That's why people go to movies, to Starbucks, to Disney World. Their primary focus is on what they are going to feel.

In the Transformation Economy, it's different. People pay for who they expect to become as a result of a series of experiences. They buy a new identity.

Back to Maslow's Hierarchy of Needs: This is where both self-identity and corporate identity come into play. In the corporate world, the CEOs are asking, *"How are you going to help our company transform? How are you going to help our company adjust to the market? How are you going to help our company become what we want to become?"*

Experience Economy
> *I pay for what I expect to feel. I buy a feeling.*

Transformation Economy
> *I pay for who I expect to become. I buy a new identity.*

A practice for B2B CEOs to gain these insights is the executive-level Customer Advisory Board. Here, the CEO of the selling company can hear directly from the CEOs of their client companies. In these small intimate settings, the CEO of the host company can build trusting relationships and ultimately gain deep understanding of what matters to the customer CEOs personally and professionally. And because these CEOs hold the vision for what their companies are out to achieve, they also have the clearest understanding of what they want their organizations to become in the future. Again, look to the agency director in a previous example who wanted to transform the agency in a certain way before he left.

From Self-Identity to Corporate Identity

While Pine and Gilmore focused on aspects of self-identity (critical in the B2C world), we have chosen to expand on that idea to the concept of corporate identity, which is more applicable in the B2B space.

A company's identity may be very broad. In some cases, the company's employees, customers and vendors all have very different ideas of the identity of the company. This can obviously pose some difficult challenges, and the less cohesiveness, clarity and focus there is in a company's identity, the less likely the company is to succeed.

Some of our clients ask employees in their employee surveys to give their own explanation of the company's mission statement. We supplement this information where needed with interviews and questionnaires to reveal how broad and diluted the company's identity really is. We use this research in our training to help the company build a single identity across all employees so the brand experience for employees and customers is consistent.

For example, if I believe the company I work for is committed to X, Y and Z, and that it produces A, B, and C, and the employee sitting next to me believes something completely different, then we are going to potentially be working with cross purposes because at the end of the day, a business is nothing more than the set of beliefs we hold and act on.

Consider this example that Tony used when he was leading the Guest and Meeting Planner Experience Programs for Gaylord Hotels.

Gaylord Hotels is a business that owns hotels, and ran them before Marriott bought the management rights. Gaylord Opryland is one of these hotels. It's a big building. The only reason it is a hotel is because of the intention to make it a hotel. It has lots and lots of rooms, 2,888 to be precise. It could be a hospital or a dormitory or any other number of entities. But the reality is, it's a hotel because that is what someone intended it to be. It's how the assets of the massive building are leveraged to create a business.

In this business, they invite people in. They have systems for getting people registered. They feed the guests and offer them comfy beds in which to rest their tired bodies. The building itself is not the Opryland Hotel, but rather, it is designated that until such point when someone decides to change it.

The truth is, a business only exists in our mind. It doesn't exist in reality in a way that we can touch it. It's not tangible. Yes, the assets of a company are tangible, and we can transfer or do all kinds of other things with the assets. The people in the business are what's real. But the moment that an employee walks out the door and into another business, they are no longer an employee of the business. They are not the business. A business is nothing more than an idea and an ideal.

And this is why, as mentioned above, the CEO needs the insights that are only garnered from an executive-to-executive level initiative such as a Customer Advisory Board. The CEO is the one who sets what the ideas and ideals of a business are. It has to come from the top down. If it comes from the bottom up, which it sometimes does, it's not governed or within the guardrails of what comes from the top down. This result is conflict among the ranks, conflict between the silos, and friction between divisions. It's up to the CEO to erect the guardrails by saying, *"Here's the kind of company we are."*

Companies cannot make decisions; the executives of a company can make decisions. The people who work for a company can make decisions. Customers of the company can make decisions. Software that runs companies, which is ultimately programmed or managed by a person, can make decisions, but the company itself cannot make decisions.

The Transformation Economy

Remember our explanation of the various economies with regard to coffee? Well, let's take it a step further and show how the coffee example progresses to the Transformation Economy.

A London-based coffee company, Change Please, helps homeless, unemployed people in various cities by hiring them to work as baristas in their mobile coffee stations. The baristas are trained to work the mobile coffee station and as a result, they get a portion of the revenue generated by the coffee sales.

This is transformational. You could go to Starbucks and get your $5 cup of coffee or you could get your $5 cup of coffee from these coffee carts. What's the difference? Well, yes, Starbucks does some good philanthropic work, but they have really built their brand around experience. Additionally, some Starbucks patrons enjoy the status of carrying around a Starbucks cup that implies that they are of the means to purchase expensive coffee. They've "made it." They think to themselves, *"This is how I want others to see me."* (It's worth noting that some people have the opposite reaction to this display of affluence.) We will go deeper into this idea of how self-concept impacts buying decisions later.

The Change Please company is transformational because they give money back directly to the less fortunate among us who are living on the streets. The choice becomes to walk down the street with a cup of Starbucks, which carries one message, or walk down the street with a Change Please coffee cup, which carries an entirely different message. Same product. Same price. Very different motives behind the buying decision.

When I walk down the street with a cup of Change Please coffee, I know, and I may want others to know that I've been a philanthropist. I helped give a homeless person a job. I'm helping a homeless person get off the street by buying this cup of coffee, which is different perception-wise from what Starbucks is doing. Yes, Starbucks creates jobs, too, but the way that they message it is vastly different. Change Please is selling, *"We help homeless people get off the street."* They are selling transformation. The product is actually irrelevant. They could sell this same message with any other product. The product is incidental to the change that's happening.

Here's another example, more closely aligned with B2B2C than the B2C example above.

Nestle announced in 2017 that by 2020 they would have 100 percent cage-free egg production.

"One could argue that brands are no longer able to influence their desired markets, but that consumers are now directly informing brands of what they want. Instead of companies inventing disruption, they are being told by their audience to meet a specific demand. Some may refer to this as the "feedback economy," and this feedback and the changes it produces is picking up steam."

~Katie McBeth, Boss Magazine January 2018

What's significant, as we go back to our conversation about generational differences, is that again, the younger generations are telling companies to meet their specific demands. Young vegans are influencing their parents to stop purchasing some brands and shifting to other brands or to other product types. They are creating a demand in the market that the market is finally responding to, but did not prophesy.

For example, the dairy industry is being hurt tremendously by the Gen Z's. Their decisions to drink more soy or almond milk and eat more plant-based food are shifting an entire industry. The Nestle decision is evidence that the impact for industries in significant.

The growth of the middle class in China is putting a strain on pork production (they eat 56 million tons of it a year) and on the agricultural system that has to scale up to meet the demand. The Chinese government responded in 2016 by creating a plan to cut pork consumption in half. Former California Governor Arnold Schwarzenegger was part of the media campaign urging the Chinese people to help the planet by eating less meat. Now a number of startup companies are seeking approval from the Chinese government to sell meatless pork options.

Due to demand for more vegan and vegetarian options, McDonald's introduced the McVegan burger in Sweden and Finland in December 2017. The company cited a U.N. statistic that 14.5 percent of greenhouse gases are the result of livestock farming. Reducing the company's impact on the environment was part of the reason they claimed they were introducing the vegan option, although it is likely they responded to the demands of the market. This seems to be a logical explanation since ten percent of the new food products in Sweden in 2017 were vegan and the global market for vegan-labeled foods was $12.8 billion in 2016.

> *"As many as 50% of consumers now are seeking more plant-based foods in their diet and 40% are open to reducing their traditional meat consumption."*
>
> ~Paul Grimwood
> CEO of Nestle USA

So, as you can see, disruption is the result of more than innovation. It stems from the human experience and points to the emergence of the Transformation Economy. Consumers are attempting to satisfy needs higher up on Maslow's Hierarchy. The examples above demonstrate that since we have an abundance of food, large segments of the population now believe they have a moral imperative to protect animals and/or to protect the environment. This is a form of belonging to something bigger than self and a form of self-actualization. CEOs need prophets who can foresee these transformations before they happen.

A PROPHET ARRIVES
The Bounce Back Story of Weight Watchers

It was 2014 and James Chambers, CEO of Weight Watchers International, knew his kingdom was in trouble. He told analysts, *"The biggest challenge we face in our business continues to be recruitment, as competitive forces continue to impact our current consumer offerings with mobile apps and activity monitors garnering a large amount of consumer and media attention and negatively impacting our consumer trial."*

The brand was ripe for repositioning, and it had to happen fast. He told Wall Street analysts that the company had to focus on strengthening *"the human connections that make a weight-loss journey more successful, connections between members, and between members and service providers."* Weight Watchers' in-person meetings were not the problem. It was the lack of human connection through digital channels. Their competition had seized on this opportunity and left Weight Watchers in the last decade.

Challenges continued throughout 2014, which was marked by upheaval for the fifty-year-old company. The Senior Vice President of Marketing left and was replaced by Lesya Lysyj, who served in the role on an interim basis while the company conducted a search for the new head of marketing. During her brief stint in the role, Lysyj cut ties with McCann Erickson, the marketing agency of record for the previous seven years. She replaced McCann Erickson with Wieden + Kennedy, yet did so without a formal review process. She instructed them to work on the winter 2015 campaigns, a significant assignment since traditionally Weight Watchers would pick up 40 percent of their new enrollees in during the winter, right after the holidays.

Just prior to the 2015 winter campaigns, and with Weight Watchers "on the brink of irrelevance," Maurice Herrera was named SVP Marketing.

Herrera's first six months were beyond tough. He later recounted that January of 2015 was one of the worst periods ever for the company. Signups were down 25 percent year-over-year, and the stock price was cut to nearly one-third while continuing to fall. Cost slashing measures were initiated which meant both his marketing budget and his team experienced deep cuts.

"I'm inspired by the mission and the transformational role that Weight Watchers plays in people's lives, and it's a privilege to become a part of it. I'm also motivated by the opportunity ahead of us to connect a whole new generation of consumers with the brand. It's a rich and complex category, and I look forward to exploring it in bold and unexpected ways."

~Maurice Herrera
SVP Marketing, Weight Watchers

Chambers and Lysyj both knew they needed a different approach to the market, so they invested in Wieden + Kennedy's "If You're Happy" campaign, and for the first time ever aired commercials during the Super Bowl. It failed miserably. As a result of the reduced number of winter signups, the shareholders predicted doom and bailed on the stock.

The one bright spot in the campaign was that it marked the beginning of a new era for the company, as the ads put the attention on "dietary challenges as a matter of psychological and behavioral compulsion" while positioning Weight Watchers as a partner to help with the hard part of losing weight. They introduced OnlinePlus and Personal Coaching, available 24/7, marking their entrance into the industry's digital landscape.

Herrera mixed things up by changing how Weight Watchers looked at marketing. He established partnerships, conducted in-depth customer research, and targeted customer-centric innovation. Additionally, he enlisted the help of existing members to inspire others to join through their stories. He also turned the messaging toward hope and aspiration, while balancing it with relatability and a holistic approach to health and wellness. Dieting alone was not enough, and before the year was out, the word "diet" was eliminated from their messaging.

"People don't want dieting and deprivation," said Gary Foster, Chief Scientific Officer at Weight Watchers. *"They want a more holistic and personalized solution, integrating healthier eating, fitness, and emotional wellbeing. They are also looking for success to be measured by more than just one number on the scale. And people tell us they want Weight Watchers to deliver more in this new, holistic world."*

In March 2015, Wieden + Kennedy was ousted, and an extensive search began for a new marketing agency. Weight Watchers also ended their long-term relationship with celebrity spokespeople including Jessica Simpson and Jennifer Hudson. This opened the door for DiMassimo Goldstein, an advertising agency focused on inspiring action, to run the spring campaigns. They were the perfect match for the new direction Herrera was taking.

It wasn't long before Lysyj, then the North American president, left the company. Before leaving she confirmed that the company wanted to create a more positive message because, *"We looked like every other offering out there, so we really had to change how we are communicating to customers."*

Herrera, now with his smaller team, engaged creative agency DiMassimo Goldstein to create a truly member-centric approach. *"We needed to create a brand identity that felt accessible and relatable as well as aspirational,"* said Herrera. That's when, with the help of talent agent, Ari Emanuel, he connected with Oprah Winfrey. After talking with Winfrey, Herrera said, *"She loved where we were going, and for her personally, she felt like this was something that she really wanted to be a part of."* Within months, Winfrey was actively involved with the marketing, even appearing in ads.

> *"Through our conversations, it became clear that there is tremendous alignment between Oprah's intention and our mission. We believe that her remarkable ability to connect and inspire people to realize their full potential is uniquely complementary to our powerful community."*
>
> ~James Chambers
> CEO, Weight Watchers

The work Herrera put in to transforming the brand led to the opportunity to create the strategic partnership with Winfrey. She went on to invest $43 million in exchange for a 10 percent stake in the company and a seat on the board. The stock soared almost immediately, up 300 percent, upon news that Winfrey invested.

"Last year [2015], we formed a strategic partnership with Oprah Winfrey, who became an investor, board member, adviser, and member of Weight Watchers," said Herrera, *"That partnership has helped us to accelerate the business and brand transformation path we've been on since 2013."*

But the honeymoon bliss wouldn't last for the shareholders. A year later, nearly all of the market value created by the "Oprah Effect" had been wiped out due to the continued exodus of members and the resulting decline in revenue.

At the end of his first year with Weight Watchers, Herrera announced that in addition to their work with DiMassimo Goldstein, they had also *"engaged Havas Worldwide in the U.S. to develop work for a winter 2016 advertising campaign aimed at driving member recruitment and bringing to life our new program innovation."* But that relationship didn't last long and DiMassimo Goldstein took the lead for the next few years.

Herrera's work as a prophet who listened to the customers reached Chambers. He told the press that Weight Watchers was, *"meeting members where they are today, inspiring and guiding healthier choices not only to lose weight but to realize benefits that go beyond just the number on the scale."*

The new program took a radical departure from the previous calorie-counting approach. They focused on healthy eating and fitness. Their app, FitBreak, provided 70 options to get movement credits. It made healthy living easier by gamifying it, triggering positive emotions and rewarding engagement. Winfrey even reported losing 40 pounds on the new system.

But by the end of 2015, the company had suffered 11 consecutive quarters of revenue declines. Membership was down 38 percent from 2013. The digital competition took a serious piece of the pie and they were not backing down.

Herrera, Winfrey and DiMassimo Goldstein redoubled their efforts and partnered more closely in 2016. They launched the "Better Together" campaign in May. But, that did not seem to be enough to create positive results for the second quarter and by the end of September, Chambers resigned as CEO. The stock fell to levels near where it had been prior to when Winfrey became an investor, with earnings for the first half of 2016 even lower than the poor results for the same period in 2015.

On the outside, it appeared the "Oprah Effect" was a bubble and that she had lost. It looked like Herrera had bet wrong and could not reposition the brand. Analysts had little hope for the company.

That's when everything changed.

Like bamboo that grows underground for years before it peeks through the surface, brand transformations take time, persistence and grit. They are not easy because the leadership in the company must transform, too. The people working on the front lines of the company must transform. The transformation needs a prophet, in this case Herrera, and a CEO who can hear the unfiltered voice of the customer, as Chambers did before he departed.

Before the door closed behind him, Chambers led the company to its first quarter of growth in years. Subscribers were up in the third quarter of 2016 by 10.1 percent compared with the prior year. It took nearly two years of disciplined effort and prophesying by Herrera, but what seemed impossible finally transpired.

Winfrey and Herrera entered the winter of 2017 working together with DiMassimo Goldstein on the "Live Fully" campaign, in which Weight Watchers promised to help members *live the life they want, full of the great foods, people and experiences they love, and the energy that comes with good health,"* It built upon the "Beyond the Scale" program from the prior year. Winfrey appeared in at least three ads in the campaign where she revealed her own story of losing over 40 pounds, and then connected with real members who shared their stories. *"This is more than what we had done last year [2016] as far as really having Oprah as a part of the campaign,"* Herrera said.

Three years after Herrera came on board, DiMassimo Goldstein recognized their joint success in a blog post: *"Together, with Herrera and his team, we've taken one of the country's most historic brands and brought them back into the national spotlight, leading to seven consecutive seasons of brand growth."* The impact was notable and measurable. In the second quarter of 2017, Weight Watchers posted earnings of $0.67 per share and revenue of $342 million, beating analyst predictions.

Herrera continued to prophesy the future while speaking at the

Association of National Advertisers (ANA) conference in 2017. He shared new initiatives that were happening including Weight Watchers cruises, bridal and mom-focused conferences, a line of cookware and portion-controlled meal delivery.

The recipe for the Weight Watchers comeback includes long-term strategic vision, unfiltered listening to the customers, executive commitment, collaboration, and a deep understanding of the human experience.

CHAPTER 2
THE SCIENCE OF HUMAN EXPERIENCE

"Breathe!"

"Breathe!"

"Breathe!"

Tony told himself as he anxiously waited for his medication to take effect. He was in anaphylactic shock in his hotel room. His wife was asleep next to him and his two young daughters were sound asleep across the room on the pullout sofa.

"Will I wake up? Will I ever see them again?"

Tears streamed down Tony's cheeks.

He had awakened moments before, gasping for air. He had to tell himself to breathe because his body was deep into shock already and his nervous system was shutting down. His heart was slowing down. He was quickly losing consciousness.

In the moments before, he had just enough strength to will himself to grab his medicine off the nightstand beside him and take it.

In that moment he made a decision. Then all he remembered was...blackness.

Defining Moments

Nearly everyone can point to at least one 'defining moment' in their lives where they decided to change the direction their life or where their business was headed. These moments cause ripple effects throughout their families, communities and eventually, possibly even the world.

Tony's decision in that defining moment was, if he lived through the night, to leave his stressful corporate job and to start his own customer experience consulting practice. As a result, he's helped clients and met people from around the world that he would likely have never crossed paths with otherwise. And, because of the impact his work has had on his clients' customer experiences, he's had an impact on the lives of hundreds of millions of customers. For some of these people, it may have been a moment that transformed their day. But for others, Tony knows it transformed their lives because his clients have shared the stories their customers told.

These moments, no matter how long, are significant because as we change by the deliberate decisions we make or by the default reactions to stimuli within or around us, in response to an experience we have, we change the course of human history. If Tony did not make the decision to leave his corporate job that fateful night many years ago, this book would not exist because it is highly likely that we would never have met.

This is as true in our personal lives as it is in our businesses. Even the seemingly small decisions we make every day can change our behaviors. Our new behaviors can change our results. Our results create a ripple effect that we can never fully comprehend. And, it all starts with a moment of human experience. Decisions contain an immeasurable potential power to change the world. Through the actions of their employees and leaders or through the influence they have on the experiences of their customers, companies share in this power.

Steve Jobs alluded to this in his 2005 commencement address at Stanford when he said,

---

"You can't connect the dots looking forward; you can only connect them looking backwards. So you have to trust that the dots will somehow connect in your future. You have to trust in something – your gut, destiny, life, karma, whatever. Because believing that the dots will connect down the road will give you the confidence to follow your heart even when it leads you off the well worn path; and that will make all the difference."

What is Human Experience?

Human experience is not something easily defined, even though we all have a basic understanding of the reference.

Experience is more than just what we feel. It's more accurately defined as our reality. It's the fullness of a moment or an extended series of moments that we weave together into a story. It is our story. No one else can ever truly understand what we experienced, but a well-told story may help them share in a part of our experience.

Human experience can involve a multitude of emotions, a multitude of thoughts or a recognition of change from who we were to who we are now. It's the awareness of the passing of time.

To experience something, to have a connection with it, to be able to say we had a particular experience, we have to be consciously aware. Our conscious awareness is what makes it an experience.

Experience vs. Influence

We may remember something as a "bad experience." The bad experience is really nothing more than the association of an unpleasant feeling with our thoughts about or memories of the experience. We may have expected something different, and when the experience didn't meet our expectations, it felt unpleasant. Or, we may have stimulated an unpleasant emotion and that feeling colored the whole experience.

When things happen, we naturally start to correlate these thoughts and feelings with the environment around us, and we try to create a cause and effect story about why we're feeling the way we feel. We do this to rationalize the irrational. This is where experience and consciousness meet.

Human beings have the ability to feel things. The moment we feel something and become aware that we are feeling something, we are then having an experience. Experience includes feelings but it is more than this.

Information flow is always going through our nervous system to our brain. We have hundreds of millions of bits of information rushing up into our brain every second from every cell of our bodies, every second of every day, but only a fraction of this information actually gets through to our conscious awareness. Physicists, neuroscientists, and psychologists debate exactly how much information we are consciously aware of, but the differences are insignificant because the gap between the conscious and subconscious processing rates is so vastly different. One estimate, shared by Dr. Joe Dispenza, is that 1 out of every 200,000,000 bits of information we absorb actually makes it to our conscious brain. We never really actually experience the remaining information because it is not available to us in a conscious way. We can never say of most of the information that rushes through our brain, *"This is what I experienced,"* because we remain unaware of it.

But when we do actually experience something, we have the experience combined with the story we tell ourselves about the experience. Think about the scenario of a car accident. The officer on the scene may get multiple interpretations of the exact same event. We each had an experience and a story we tell ourselves about the experience. The actual experience is what we are aware of thinking and feeling, and then there's the story we tell ourselves about why. We construct our story from only the extremely limited details we are aware of.

Because it requires conscious awareness to experience something, and because we only process a limited amount of information consciously, and because we have millions and millions of bits of information being processed by our subconscious mind, we are open to being influenced by many other unknown and unknowable factors.

Let's assume for a moment that you are having a really great experience in a restaurant and decide to tip the server extra. You're consciously aware of feeling really good. You may say, *"This is a great server. This was a really great experience."* When someone asks you why it was so great, you have to then try to figure that out.

You may have been influenced by the server's disposition. Perhaps he gave you a compliment, or repeated your order back to you, or snuck in a few extra mints at the end of the meal. It could have been one of hundreds of other influences that remain nestled in your subconscious mind.

The reality for you is that you had a great experience in a restaurant. The why is often very hard to get to because of the vast number of possible influences. It's the influence that moves an experience we have in a particular direction, but we may never be able to consciously point accurately to a specific reason why an experience was as it was.

Little things can influence an experience but the influence is not the experience. You can, however, use influence to evoke experiences. A customer service team offering help is not the same as customer experience. The offer of help may trigger an experience. An experience is what the customer has uniquely themselves, the causes of which they may or may not be able to describe with accuracy.

Experiences and the influences that trigger those experiences matter significantly in business because they impact how we decide and what we decide.

THE AWAKENING OF AN INDUSTRY
Casper: The Success Story of a Startup

How many startups do you know that can generate $1 million in their first month? Or better yet, how many startups do you know that can generate $20 million in the first 10 months, and ultimately drive a valuation of $555 million in less than two years?

Well, it happened. It happened with Casper, a New York-based startup run by a band of five millennials determined from the outset to disrupt a $14 billion industry.

Grounded in the value of simplicity, this innovative maker of sleep products grew the company by creating an experience for their customers that isn't a pain in the neck. Selling only one model of their mattress, selling it online direct-to-consumers, and offering 100 days to try it out and if not satisfied, issuing a full refund, has flipped the traditional mattress-buying model on its side.

Wait. Online direct-to-consumers?

Yes, that's right. Casper delivers their mattresses in a mini-fridge sized box, complete with a branded cutting tool to slice open the packaging.

The customer no longer has to deal with overzealous commissioned sales reps or 30 versions of memory foam, latex or pillow top mattresses from which to choose. Not only that, rather than basing an expensive purchasing decision on a mere two minutes of trying it out, the company will come pick up the mattress from your home if you are not completely satisfied within 100 days. But the cherry on top is that the mattresses are priced lower than many competitors, ranging from $500 for a twin to $950 for a king.

While everyone is a potential target since everyone sleeps (or at least tries to), this group of entrepreneurs has chosen to zero in on the younger generation, heavily leveraging social media and city transportation advertising to reach prospects. They have gone away from messaging to the traditional target market of individuals in their 40s and 50s and rather seek established communities in which to tell their story such as podcast listeners and commuters.

"Most people in their 20s and 30s don't have problems with sleep, don't have back issues," says CEO Phillip Krem. *"And yet the industry got caught up with marketing that's like, 'Solve your back pain with this product.' We wanted to get away from that kind of product solution-type marketing."*

Because they are committed to the spirit of community, they have a laser focus not on just selling products but rather building lifelong relationships. Less than 20 percent of their social media content directly promotes their products, which now includes pillowcases, sheets and dog mattresses, creating a vocal legion of ambassadors for their brand.

"Early on, we wanted our customers to be the voice of growing Casper to the greatest degree possible," said co-founder T. Luke Sherwin. *"When you convince someone to buy a mattress on the Internet, to us they have secondary value in convincing their friends to do the same. By virtue of liking Casper and interacting with our fun posts, they might inspire other people to refer their friends to Casper and give them the tool kit, and that was really primary for us."*

Going for the long-term relationship, Casper looks for engagement over experience.

"To me, "experience" is saying that there's a duration to how you interact with our brand, but with us there are multiple touch points," Sherwin stated. *"I think Casper looks at the original purchase as the beginning of a relationship, and not the end of the experience."*

Valued at over $750 million in late 2017, the company shows no signs of slowing down, having partnered with Target to sell their sheets and pillow cases in all of their retail locations and online.

The odds of their rocket ship trajectory and enormous financial success are not lost on members of the founding team. *"I mean, it's mind-blowing,"* says Krem. *"We just celebrated our millionth customer interaction—it's just crazy how many people look for us, how many people sleep on our products."*

It says a lot about a company that could boast about their huge financial numbers but rather chooses to focus on the number of customer interactions.

HUMAN DECISIONS

"A good decision is based on knowledge, not numbers."

~Plato
Greek philosopher, educator

Imagine you leave the office and are headed home for the evening when your significant other calls to ask you to stop at the store to pick up a bottle of wine, but leaves the decision of which type and brand up to you. When you get to the store, you browse the rows and make your selection. You pay and drive home. Did you make this decision with full awareness of your decision-making criteria, or did you have unknown influences acting upon you?

Researchers have been studying the effect of ambient music on shoppers' decisions and behaviors since at least the 1980s. In one published study, researchers alternated playing French and German music in a wine store. When the French music played, sales were higher on French wines. When the German music played, German wines outsold the French wines. The kicker is that the shoppers reportedly were unaware of the background music. The subconscious influence of the music affected their decisions, but they had no conscious awareness of even experiencing the music.

While this is a business book, everything we discuss will be better understood and applied with a foundational knowledge of the human experience. Businesses succeed or fail based upon the quality of the decisions made by the humans engaged with the business.

The essence of the CEO's job is to make decisions, and with that, he depends on the senior leaders to provide him with enough information to make good ones that will drive the company in the right direction. Unfortunately, sometimes decisions are consciously made based upon nothing more than graphs, charts and filtered data, not inclusive of the other factors that are grounded in the concepts behind human experience. Often there is little consideration given to the subconscious influences that may be impacting the decisions or the decision making process.

Every member of every organization makes decisions every day. What influences these decisions? Who influences these decisions? How can we make better decisions? What plays into the decisions that are made by the customers? How can we influence the decisions made by the customers? These are all questions that can be addressed by having a deeper understanding of the human experience.

Let's start by how we view "experience." As we previously discussed, experience includes the emotions we are consciously aware of (i.e. we feel), the thoughts we think and the stories we tell. Our experiences impact our personal and professional decisions through what we feel, what we think about what we feel, and what we feel about what we think. Experience can be both a cause and an effect of our thoughts and feelings. It is the cause of our expectations of an event and it is the effect of how we evaluate an event.

Tying this into decision-making, our decisions are affected primarily through our emotions. Most emotions never rise to the level of a feeling because they sit just outside our conscious awareness. These subconscious emotions can profoundly influence our decisions as shown in the wine shopping experiment described above. These emotions could be triggered by physiological states (hunger, fatigue, pain), by external conditions (the environment, external stimuli) or by psychological states (feelings, the thoughts about our feelings and the feelings about our thoughts.) This is true of all humans.

The experience you're consciously having and the emotions you're subconsciously processing in a moment affect the decisions you're making in that moment.

Moments of Decision

Any given moment in a person's life has the potential to change the course of human history.

An "Aha!" moment can shift a person's entire worldview. Even a one-degree shift can move someone down a completely different path. It can alter the course of a business, of a relationship, and of a life. It has the power to change the world because it impacts the person and those around him. This is universally applicable in business, whether B2B, B2C, B2B2C, or employer to employee. Why? Because we are all humans.

Yes, we oftentimes make decisions based on budgets, economics, market conditions, etc., but basically, decision makers are humans having a human experience. Typically, there are emotions associated to the rational factors of decision-making. As humans, we cannot entirely eliminate emotion from our decision-making processes.

It is far more advantageous for a business to build upon a foundation of the human experience rather than simply the user experience, employee experience or customer experience. By setting aside the labels of user/customer/employee and replacing them with "human," a deeper level of understanding results and better business outcomes are realized.

We have experiences with which we build our belief systems on how the world operates. We have experiences that we interpret through our belief systems that cause us to set our expectations, change our expectations, or change our memories of an experience.

It may seem outlandish, but we've found that as few as three words in a call center script at the time of booking the reservation can influence a guest's multi-day experience at a resort. And, we've learned that we can detect a guest's price sensitivity based on if they choose to use the word "resort" or "hotel" and how they use the word in their online reviews.

Fundamentally, if we can tap into the human experience someone else is having in a specific moment, and if we can tap into the emotions they are feeling in this moment, we can affect how they experience the world. We can positively affect how they think. For example, with this focus on the human experience, we can help change the thinking of someone who feels they can't land a big client or succeed in their business. Or, we can create impact in a moment when an employee goes well above the call of duty for a customer and creates a positive, long-lasting interpretation of that gesture.

Tony's experience of a life-or-death moment gave him the gift of reassessing his priorities instantly. The feelings and thoughts were so intense that it aligned his desire to live a long life with his wife and to be an active part of his daughters' lives. This moment holds deep meaning for him because he made a decision to change his worldview and how he viewed himself. Rather than seeing himself as an employee, he began to see himself as a business owner. Rather than allow himself to consider what would happen if he died, he decided to make a decision about what he would do with the rest of his life. And, that decision led him, or us, here.

The Business Case for Human Experience

"I've learned that people will forget what you said, people will forget what you did, but people will never forget how you made them feel."

~Maya Angelou
poet, singer, civil rights activist

This classic quote remains timeless as it relates to the human experience, but let's change it up a bit to address it in a business context.

"I've learned that people will forget what your business said, people will forget what your business did, but people will never forget how your business made them feel."

Yep, that works.

Now more than ever, businesses are evolving from the concept of Customer Experience (CX) to Human Experience (HX), and for good and valid reasons. Bottom line: Customers are human and have experiences that mirror that humanity, including how they feel.

Forward thinking companies are beginning to realize that while Net Promoter and customer satisfaction scores are good lag measures for monitoring how they are doing, the real measure of a company's future success is much harder to gauge because at the core is how the customer actually *feels and what she remembers*. How each customer's life circumstances, desires, aspirations, needs and perspectives play into their experience with your products and services is not easily dropped into a weekly report with fancy charts and graphs.

Some experts or customer experience practitioners may suggest that we can use speech or text analysis and quantify the emotions customers are feeling when they speak or write. With more than a decade of building customer feedback analysis programs for award-winning voice of the customer departments that leverage advanced speech and text analytics, we can assure you that the sentiment metrics are simply not up to the task and are insufficient to communicate the depth and richness of human experience.

Diving into human experience can be tricky, as there is so much involved including emotions, psychology, interpretation, frame of reference, influences, conscious vs. subconscious, etc., all of which make predicting and orchestrating customer happiness quite difficult. But like many other things in business and in life, when there is focus on something, it tends to grow.

Just Google "human experience in business" and you will find countless articles that explore the evolution of this line of thinking. When you think about it, a human is your customer for a very small percentage of their day, but they are human every minute of their day. While historically, companies have focused on the persona of the "customer," there is a growing trend toward focusing on the persona of the "human."

Consider this: 80 percent of brands believe they deliver great customer experiences, but according to WFA Marketers, only 8 percent of consumers agree. That's a massive disconnect.

Imagine how this statistic would change if the companies doing the marketing were actually tapped into the human experience of the customer rather than the traditional customer experience. Aligning not just what customers do or how they feel for a few moments of their day when acting as a customer, but more pointedly, what these actions and feelings mean for the person as a human being has a dramatic impact on the things companies value most, including loyalty, referrals, and overall connection to the company brand.

REDEFINING HAPPINESS

"Not getting it wrong does not remotely equal getting it right."

~Dr. Martin Seligman
psychologist, educator, author

The Fundamental Problem in the CX Industry

The customer experience industry has contributed immensely to the improvement of the quality of life for millions, maybe even billions of people. Unless we are blinded by ideology, we can definitely say that we are better off today than we were 30 or 50 years ago as customers. That may not mean we are satisfied with what we have today, but we are better off.

While we can make this statement unequivocally, we can with equal vigor state that the vast majority of people in the customer experience industry are following fundamentally flawed foundational principles. As such, they will never be able to achieve what is really possible through customer experience and their companies will not achieve their full potential.

In nearly every conversation customer experience experts have, they quickly turn toward their favorite score and they dig into company product, policies, procedures, processes or people skills to see how they can improve these scores. This is their mistake. However, this is a mistake that is not necessarily their fault. The industry has perpetuated the focus on solving problems in a manner similar to the approach the quality movement used in the 1990s. They start with the company, not with a proper understanding of the human person.

Some may counter that there is a trend now to talk about "customer happiness." In reality, this is usually just a catchy way of saying "customer service" or "customer experience." So, let's look at what the real, hardcore science of happiness tells us. (Yes, there is a science of happiness.)

Shawn Achor, world-renowned happiness researcher, gave a TED talk, which happens to be one of the most popular TED talks online. Since May 2011 the video has accumulated over 17 million views on Ted.com alone. Here is what he said about predicting happiness.

"If I know everything about your external world, I can only predict 10 percent of your long-term happiness. 90 percent of your long-term happiness is predicted not by the external world, but by the way your brain processes the world."

This statement may shock you. If you are in the business of "customer happiness," it better shock you. It means that no matter what we do with the product, policies, processes, procedures and people skills in our companies, we can only have a minimal impact on the long-term happiness (real happiness) of our customers.

What's worse, most measures of customer experience are really not measures of happiness at all. Customer satisfaction, recommendations (net promoter score), customer effort score, and others, have minimal if any foundation in psychological sciences. More and more studies are showing that these metrics may only be predictive or useful in particular situations. It is clear, there is no metric that works for all or even most companies and industries.

Before you rush to your email or LinkedIn to send us a nastygram and tell us that your metric works well, read the first sentence of this chapter again.

"The customer experience industry has contributed immensely to the improvement of the quality of life for millions, maybe even billions of people."

We really believe this.

The customer experience industry has its roots deep in the foundations of the quality movement of the 1980s and 1990s with Lean Manufacturing, Total Quality Management, Six Sigma and Theory of Constraints. The metrics we mentioned above do help companies improve in many cases because they help the company pick a north star by which to guide their investment decisions. And, like investments in the quality movement, these investments pay off sometimes.

But, if we want to be intellectually honest, and if we really want to unlock the power and potential of the moments of human experience that our customers have with our companies, products and services, then we need to admit the truth. Quality is important and essential. But the quality movement is not sufficient to create a deep and lasting impact on human perception, human experience, human decision-making and human existence. We need something more.

One of the anchors of the quality movement that holds customer experience back from progress is the same anchor that held psychology back for over 100 years from focusing how to help humans flourish. In a 2004 interview, Dr. Martin Seligman, the founder of positive psychology, said:

"For 30 years I did trauma, helplessness, depression, the negative emotions and how to relieve them. Then I found myself the President of the American Psychological Association and I thought what I should do is ask, 'What's wrong with psychology?' When I looked around I found a 100 to 1 ratio on the number of articles about depression and the number [of articles about the] science about happiness.

"So it seemed very important to me, particularly in a time of wealth and prosperity, that the part of psychology that's been unbaked, the part about 'What are the best things in life? What takes life beyond going from minus 8 to minus 2 when we lie awake at night? How do we go from plus 2 to plus 5 in our lives?' So, 5 years ago I acquired the mission of asking the question and trying to support the science of 'What are the positive emotions? How do we build them? What are the strengths and virtues? How do we build those? And, what are the positive institutions? And, how do we build those?'"

We opened this chapter with a quote from Seligman. It is highly relevant right here. We've seen, too many customer experience professionals and the CEOs and executives they work for believe that if we simply stop getting things wrong, that that is reciprocal to getting things right. If we stop annoying customers, they will be happy. But, as we'll show later, Prospect Theory proves this premise grossly inaccurate and completely inadequate as a fundamental belief on which to base your customer experience management strategies.

If we have not been clear enough, let us repeat it again: Happiness is not the result of an absence of disappointment, anger, frustration or other unpleasant emotions. It is something of an entirely different dimension.

So, let's look at what happiness is, according to the scientists.

What Happiness Is

When the average person says they are happy, they often mean they are cheerful, upbeat, and even joyful. These are, in actuality, only a part of happiness. Positive or pleasant emotions are things we seek out for their own sake. We enjoy them while we feel them. When they are gone, we seek experiences that will help us feel them again. These are often the feelings we associate with a positive customer experience. After all, we measure satisfaction and we tell our teams to "surprise and delight" our customers.

When Seligman and his team of researchers dared to ask, *"What more there might be in life than not suffering,"* they discovered five endeavors that human beings, when not oppressed, engage in. These they call PERMA.

Seligman's PERMA model

The language used by Seligman is broad and covers human experience, not just customer experience, so we want to take a moment to dive into a few words that have particular meaning. "When not oppressed," may not seem relevant to you from a customer experience perspective. At first, it seemed a bit too much for us, too. But then, we had an epiphany. Try this thought experiment for yourself:

Imagine the next time you go shopping for groceries, you walk into your favorite store (assuming you're not using Amazon). You are shocked. You look around and see in every aisle that you have only 14 percent of the choices you had yesterday. How would you feel? Oppressed? Would you run to the manager and demand an answer? Would you be frustrated and threaten to go to their competitor across the street?

According to Michael Ruhlman, author of the book *"Grocery: The Buying and Selling of Food in America,"* grocery stores in the 1990s had about 7000 items. Now they have upward of 50,000. Grocery stores are not unique. B2B and B2C customers in nearly every sector have exponentially more options available today than ever before.

Oh, don't forget about the information you also have available about each of those products. Remember how in the 1990s you did not have a smartphone connected to the internet filled with sites that could tell you the ingredients you need to make that special recipe, if the product you are looking at is actually vegan, and what they really mean by "organic."

So, think about your shopping experience 20 years ago. If you were magically transported back there, knowing what you know today, would you feel oppressed? We know we would.

When your customers have the ability to make choices freely, like all humans that Seligman studied, they pursue five endeavors. These have become known as PERMA, and they are proven to lead to happiness (or as Seligman prefers, "well-being").

In his book, *"Flourish,"* Seligman describes the nature of each of these endeavors that his team proved scientifically is a part of happiness.

"Each element of well-being must itself have three properties to count as an element:

1. *It contributes to well being.*
2. *Many people pursue it for its own sake, not merely to get any of the other elements.*
3. *It is defined and measured independently of the other elements."*

To better understand your customers, let's look at the five types of experiences they are seeking.

P = POSITIVE EMOTIONS

We are most familiar in customer experience with the positive or pleasant emotions. Satisfaction, surprise and delight, and ease of doing business are all versions of pleasant emotions. When you consider human experience more broadly, we might include cheerfulness, joy, amusement, awe, inspiration and more. These emotions make up the pleasant life.

Companies spend fortunes trying to figure out how to trigger the pleasant emotions. Whether it is Disney or Vegas where they create a facade that customers accept and willingly engage with, or if it is your local Costco offering tasty samples on a Saturday morning, we are barraged with sensory stimuli to distract us from reality and to focus our attention on a particular feeling that motivates us to behave as the company desires. As we previously discussed, these sensory and emotional stimuli are the primary focus of the Experience Economy so we create positive memories. These positive experiences correlate with higher spending in the moment and the positive memories correlate with higher lifetime value and more recommendations or referrals.

What is not widely discussed, in our race to stay top of memory, is that there are three fundamental flaws with an economy or a business strategy based on the triggering of positive feelings. These flaws are the result of human biology and threaten the companies and the economy as a whole if we do not address them by pivoting to new and better strategies. We will explore these flaws in detail below, but here's a brief overview:

1. Emotions are not just positive and negative; they are multidimensional and complex.
2. Emotionality is heritable, so people react differently to influences and interpret their experiences differently.
3. The desire to seek positive emotions puts us on a hedonic treadmill.

It's important to note that while having stories from customers who are filled with positive emotions for your product, service and brand, the real learning for an organization comes from the customers who may not have had a positive experience and who are willing to express to you why.

In Betsy's work building and executing Customer Advisory Boards, she coaches clients to not just seek board members who are raving fans, but rather strive for a balance of those customers along with customers who can provide insight to what's not working well. While it may feel great to hear a bunch of warm and fuzzy comments from happy customers, if it stops there it does very little to advance the organization. And taking this a step further, while it's important to hear the negative emotions that come from unhappy customers, it's even more important to actively go above and beyond to get them back to a state of exuberance about your company. We'll dive into this more when we discuss Prospect Theory later.

To understand this in a more scientific way, consider this example.

Tony was an early leader in the use of text mining software to analyze the content and sentiment of customer comments on surveys when he led the guest and meeting planner experience programs for Gaylord Entertainment, which included Gaylord Hotels. Marriott now manages Gaylord Hotels. He used one of the earliest versions of Clarabridge's text mining platform (2.x) to analyze hundreds of thousands of surveys filled out by meeting planners and guests in the hotels, retails shops, restaurants, live entertainment venues, a golf course, museum and more.

At that time, sentiment was a relatively crude measure. It essentially calculated a score based on positive or negative words and phrases. These values were either assigned by the software or by the analysts who set up the software. It proved to be helpful, but there were many challenges including the inability to distinguish sarcasm and irony from the straightforward sentiment. There were also times where surveys with very negative ratings contained words or phrases with very positive sentiment. It was always challenging to explain these apparent discrepancies to the C-Suite.

After leaving Gaylord, Tony worked with several clients to help them build their Voice of the Customer (VoC) programs. In some cases, these clients went beyond the use of surveys and analyzed emails, chat session conversations, call center notes, and even scanned letters. In these scenarios, he and the clients did not have the benefit of the self-reported ratings from customers so there was no way to instantly determine if a customer was feeling positive or negative as was possible with a survey. Because the value of sentiment as a metric was oversold, and the challenges not addressed, the clients were convinced that sentiment should be a Key Performance Indicator (KPI) and they built their reporting for the VoC programs around that belief. This is actually still a common practice in the industry.

In an effort to improve the reporting, Tony continually studied the most recent research regarding emotions and the language of emotions. Soon he realized that the problems he saw with the use of sentiment were only the tip of the iceberg.

Emotions are Complex

Emotions are not simply positive or negative. This dimension is called the emotion's valence. Emotions can also be evaluated on their ability to arouse, which means we experience a heightened state of physiological activity, like anger or fear compared to calmness or apathy. They can also be evaluated on a dimension of dominance, which indicates if they trigger an internal locus of control (high dominance) or and external locus of control (low dominance).

This three dimensional model of emotions, Valence Arousal Dominance or VAD, accounts for tremendous complexity in emotions, and it also helps us understand that not all positive emotions are equivalent. Some move us to act (high dominance) while others leave us immobile (low dominance).

How does this impact your business strategy?

If you only focus on triggering positive emotions, you may invest a fortune and only trigger positive, high arousal but low dominance emotions which cause your customers to feel good, but they have no motivation to act, to share their story or to recommend others. This means that you may have succeeded in raising your customer experience scores, but you will not harness the value of those positive feelings with an ROI that makes it worthwhile.

Not all positive emotions drive profitable behavior, which is why improving customer experience scores without considering the three dimensions of the emotions your brand is triggering is a mistake. Many companies that have all but given up on seeing an ROI from their CX programs are victims of their own lack of awareness of the complexity of human emotions. The later chapters of this book will give you ways to successfully generate an ROI in the face of these challenges that emotions present.

If the fact that emotions are multidimensional is not enough to convince you to reconsider your reliance on triggering positive emotions as your single strategy for customer experience, then you should consider the two additional flaws in your strategy that arise from the nature of emotions.

Emotions are Genetic

Emotions are heritable. According to researchers, about 40-60 percent of our emotionality is genetic. In addition, there is a distribution of how sensitive we are to emotions. About 20 percent of the population is believed to be highly sensitive. Research shows that this sensitivity is linked to a genetic variation that may cause heightened activity in specific brain regions. The neurotransmitter norepinephrine influences more intense emotional responses and sensitivity.

Rebecca Todd, lead author of the sensitivity study said, *"People really do see the world differently. For people with this gene variation, the emotionally relevant things in the world stand out much more."*

Adam Anderson, senior author of the study stated, *"Emotions are not only about how we feel about the world, but how our brains influence our perception of it. As our genes influence how we literally see the positive and negative aspects of our world more clearly, we may come to believe the world has more rewards or threats."*

Additional research studies indicate that different emotions or different aspects of emotions may be heritable to different levels. One study of twins by Martin Melchers of the University of Bonn and Elisabeth Hahn of Saarland University, found that heritability of two different subcomponents of empathy, affective empathy (a person's ability to feel what someone else is feeling) and cognitive empathy (a person's ability to understand another person's feelings and reasoning) had different levels of heritability. The affective component was 52-57 percent heritable whereas the cognitive component was only about 27 percent heritable.

What does this mean for your business?

If your strategy of building customer loyalty relies primarily or solely on triggering positive emotions to create memorable experiences, you are only going to be successful with a portion of the population. Genetics have a sizable influence on if or how much we feel emotions as well as if or how much of the environment triggers our emotions. Seligman points out in his research that even with the most effective interventions they have designed in positive psychology, the best they have been able to do is to move people up within their range of emotionality by 10-15 percent. In the end, your company will not be able to move people who are low on emotionality to a new range. At best, you will be able to help them reach a higher point in their normal range.

This also means that your dependence on satisfaction scores alone as a KPI or success metric is flawed because it does not account for human biology. A better scoring system would consider the relative change in a customer's emotionality from where they start to where they reach, but that is a topic for another book.

Emotions Require Escalation

In 1971, researchers, Brickman and Campbell, coined the term "hedonic treadmill." Michael Eysenck, a British psychologist, later modified their work. This is the third factor that puts a damper on any customer experience strategy that focuses on driving ROI solely through triggering positive emotions.

Essentially, each person has a happiness set point. At given points in time, we may feel relatively more positive or more negative, but in the long-term there is little change to our levels of happiness. Some refer to this as "hard-wiring."

As you already know, external events have very little impact on our long-term happiness. Our bodies are designed to notice relative changes. Think about your senses. You smell something different. You see shades, shadows or colors and make images from them. You hear various tones or frequencies and construct music or words from them. These are all examples of how we humans sense relative differences and make sense of the world around us. Our emotions are no different.

We feel a boost of happiness, joy or enthusiasm. The sudden change in our physiological state captures our attention for the moment while the chemical cocktail that triggered it surges through our body. But within a few minutes, the wave of emotion will fade. Dr. Joan Rosenberg, a renowned psychotherapist, has even designed an intervention based on research that emotional waves last no more than 90 seconds. Her work has had revolutionary effects on the treatment of grief, anxiety, and other unpleasant emotions. But this research also has a profound impact on customer experience because we can see that waves of feelings are very temporary.

This may be a source of good news because companies can develop tactics that help customers through the waves of negative emotions they feel when things go wrong. On the other hand, any tactics that rely on triggering waves of positive emotion are equally temporary. To continue to be successful using a customer experience strategy that relies only on evoking positive emotions, the company must find ways to continue to trigger more waves and increase the amplitude of the peak of the waves to stimulate that positive emotion. Committing to this strategy is like committing to running on a treadmill that gets a bit faster and steeper with every step. You're going to fly off eventually.

Are we destined to fail because we've failed to understand the complexity, heritability and the hedonic treadmill of positive emotions?

Not necessarily. We simply need to evolve our understanding of what customers are seeking by being aware of what helps humans flourish. This means we must look deeper into Seligman's PERMA model to understand the other elements that lead to lasting happiness.

As you proceed through the explanation of the other four elements of PERMA, ask yourself if you already leverage each element in your products, services and experiences. Consider how you might differentiate your customers' experiences by incorporating more elements and deepening the use of those elements beyond positive emotion that you may already tap into today. The prophets of today are listening carefully to their customers and discerning how their company is already and can further leverage the five elements of PERMA to create richer experiences that people remember longer and drive loyalty in ways positive emotions alone cannot.

E = ENGAGEMENT

"[Flow] refers to those moments of rapt attention and total absorption where we get so focused on the task at hand that everything else disappears."

~Steven Kotler
author, journalist, entrepreneur

Maybe your company, product or service is not one that can easily evoke positive emotions. Consider a professional sports franchise like an NBA team where over 20,000 people crowd themselves into seats, fitted closely together, with limited leg space and almost no room for people with middle seats to move easily in and out of their row while others are seated. Before the game there are long lines to enter the arena. At half-time the concession stands and restrooms have lines snaking away from them as excited fans prepare for the next half of the battle between greats. The end of the game leads to a rush through the crowded hallways to get to the parking areas so fans can leave. And, in their cars, these same fans sit waiting for their turn to exit the parking garage and slowly navigate several blocks away from the stadium to open roads.

That's what most fans experience. And, if their team loses big, all that pain feels even worse. But, for home game fans of the Cleveland Cavaliers things are a bit different. When fans on go to Google to rate their experience and share memories of attending home games in the Quicken Loans Arena, or "The Q" as it is affectionately called, they say there are "excellent seats everywhere," and that "the staff was extremely friendly and helpful." The repetition of comments like, "Good parking, fun atmosphere, good food selection with decent prices..." show how well the arena management has designed the environment to trigger a "5-star" experience.

A few years ago, I (Tony) had the opportunity to work with the operations, sales and marketing teams at The Q. While there, Mike Ostrowski, VP of Franchise Operations for the Cavaliers Operating Company, gave a pre-game tour of the arena and talked through some of the ways they create an environment for the fans. Each night had a theme. The night we met, they had family night. Kids could create their own posters, get their faces painted, meet the cheerleaders in person and more. During the game, their activities promoted a family atmosphere. The food was even focused on families with kid-friendly options at a reasonable price.

As Mike and I walked, I shared with him how what I was witnessing was really setting the stage for group flow. It was not so much about feeling good in the moment, but more about forgetting about everything except for the moment. Parents could forget about challenges at work and planning dinner. Kids could forget about the test they struggled with at school and the homework that they had to do later. Everyone could simply focus on the moment. In fact, while there were obviously positive emotions being expressed, there was much more focus on getting ready for the game.

Some kids with their tongues sticking slightly out of their mouths were creating posters with their favorite players. One mom was taking pictures of her daughter who stood like a marble statue without expression as she got her face painted by an arena employee. Dads were navigating the crowds and focused on finding the end of the fast-moving concession lines so they had dinner for their families.

A snapshot revealed an apparent paradox. An observer could see group chaos and group flow. While being totally focused on their own objectives, the individuals in the crowd moved like a school of fish on the reef. Everyone moved in unison and 20,000 people got to where they wanted to be with their snacks and fan paraphernalia as the game began. Then, for the next few hours, the crowd moved into and out of group flow. During critical moments of the game, they forgot about everything else outside the arena, their empty popcorn bucket, or the sticky soda under their feet. All that mattered was the ball reaching its mark. And, any way they could, they were going to help it get there. Fingers were crossed. Breath was held. Pompoms were shaken. Voices were raised shouting at the players, the ball, the officials...at nearly everything that was happening on the floor of the arena.

In those moments of group flow, no one who was in flow was feeling anything. It was only after the moment faded that they would feel and think about what just happened.

Thought and feeling are usually absent during the flow state, and only in retrospect do we say, *"That was fun,"* or *"That was wonderful,"* or *"Why the hell did he just do that?"*

The subjective state for pleasures, or positive emotion, is in the present. The subjective state for engagement is only retrospective because in the moment, one has no conscious capacity to feel.

Engagement is often referred to as the state of flow. Flow is not for groups only. In fact, that groups can experience flow is a relatively recent discovery. Early studies focused on athletes getting into a flow. Many refer to it as "being in the zone." Then researchers studied artists and composers while they were effortlessly creating. The Koln Concert from 1975 is a perfect example of flow when pianist Keith Jarrett performed solo on an out-of-tune piano. It became the best-selling solo jazz album in history. Some looked at how Buddhist monks or Catholic nuns entered flow while they are meditating and later reported a sense of ecstasy or oneness with nature or God. The most recent research has revealed that nearly anyone can get into flow because there are twenty known triggers.

You may be asking, *"What is flow?"*

Steven Kotler answered that in his TED talk on the subject by saying, *"Flow is a technical term and is defined as an optimal state of consciousness when we feel our best and we perform our best. More specifically, it refers to those moments of rapt attention and total absorption where we get so focused on the task at hand that everything else disappears. Action and awareness start to merge. Your sense of self vanishes. Time passes strangely. Sometimes it will slow down and you'll get a freeze-frame effect. More frequently it speeds up and five hours passes by in like five minutes. And throughout, all aspects of performance, both mental and physical, go through the roof."*

It turns out that during moments of deep engagement and optimal performance, our prefrontal cortex becomes hypoactive. Parts of it slow down or deactivate. Our ability to do long-term planning, calculate time, be aware of our self or listen to our inner critic all disappear. We experience freedom because we get out of our head and out of our way.

The state of engagement emerges when the right combination of individual or group triggers are activated. In *"Stealing Fire,"* Kotler and his co-author Jamie Wheal describe how people find ways to drive their attention into the here and now and to create an environment that produces a lot of fast feedback and sensory input. Their list of individual triggers includes: passion/purpose, risk, novelty, complexity, unpredictability, deep embodiment, immediate feedback, clear goals, challenge/skills ratio, and creativity/pattern recognition. Their list of group triggers include: close listening, shared goals, shared risk, "yes and…", complete concentration, autonomy/a sense of control, blending egos, familiarity, equal participation, and open communication.

When the right conditions are met, the body and brain of the individual becomes saturated with the five highly potent neurochemicals of norepinephrine, dopamine, anandamide, serotonin and endorphins. Together, these alter the consciousness of the individual and transform how they perceive and interact with reality.

Physical performance improves as pain is deadened and strength increased. Mental performance skyrockets as attention is focused, patterns recognition increases and new connections are made. In this information-rich conscious state of selflessness, timelessness and effortlessness, researchers have recorded average improvements in creativity, learning, motivation and productivity ranging from 200 percent to 500 percent.

Researchers and consultants are touting the value of training employees on how they can get into flow and creating environments that allow them to achieve this state more easily and maintain it longer. Done correctly, we wholeheartedly agree. The research is overwhelming showing that employee experience drives customers experience. The Temkin Group found that customer experience leaders have 1.5 times more engaged employees than customer experience laggards. Researchers from Gallup discovered that companies with highly engaged employees outperform their competitors by 147 percent. In related research, Gallup showed that nearly 70% of employees are not engaged or are actively disengaged. These employees are not adding value and may even be actively destroying value in your company while damaging the reputation of your brand and the relationships your customers have with your brand.

But we encourage you to take another step.

Remember: Some of your customers may be genetically predisposed to not feel positive emotions in the moment. And, your company cannot long afford joining the rat race of the hedonic treadmill. There is more to happiness than just feeling good in the moment.

Consider how your company, like The Q Arena, could help your customers reach the state of flow and experience their optimal state of human performance as an individual or while being one with a group.

R = RELATIONSHIP

Since at least 1995 when the term Customer Relationship Management (CRM) was coined, companies have been claiming to have relationships with their customers. Unfortunately, this is hardly true for many companies today. At best, they have a collection of data about customers, but few of the employees and likely none of the executives of any company of size really know their customers.

Knowing your customer is not the same as knowing about your customers.

No accumulation of facts will ever equal a relationship. For this reason, Tony dug deep to understand what the foundation of a relationship with a person is. After extensive research he concluded that a shared experience between people seems to be the basis for every relationship. That's why this element of PERMA, positive relationships, is particularly fascinating in light of today's race to remove human employees and replace them with technology. It's as if companies think that automated personalization of a user experience is somehow better than an authentic moment of human connection. It is this social connection that helped our species and other species with a hive mindset, like ants and bees, thrive. Together we are stronger. Apart we die.

One of the easiest industries to study the impact of shared experiences is the hospitality industry. Technology has led to many disruptions in the industry. Sites like TripAdvisor.com and apps like Airbnb have altered the competitive landscape for travelers seeking overnight accommodations by providing transparency and ubiquitous access to data about locations, amenities and rates, as well as guest reviews. You might consider the technology inside the hotels as disruptive too. From high speed WiFi, keyless entry, and mobile check-in, the industry's baseline is continually shifting. Yet, as fast as technology is advancing, the biggest disruption is not caused by technology per se.

We've noticed that there is a quiet but steady shift in the hotels ranked in the top five of nearly every market we've studied on TripAdvisor.com. While it would seem that capital investments in building, staffing and operating 4-star or 5-star hotels and resorts would ensure they reach and maintain a top ranking, this has not been the case. While writing this section of the book, we reviewed the hotels ranked in the top five for the five largest U.S. cities.

Each of these cities has a number of hotels and resorts rated by experts as 4 and 5-star properties. However, in four of the five cities, hotels with expert ratings of 2.5, 3.0 and 3.5 were solidly positioned in the top five and easily outranking several 4 and 5-star hotels.

City	Hotel	TripAdvisor Hotel Rank	Expert Rating (Stars)	Average Guest Rating Out of 5
New York City	414 Hotel	#3 of 480	3.5	4.5
Los Angeles	Magic Castle	#2 of 430	3.5	4.5
	Hollywood Orchid Suites	#4 of 430	2.5	4.5
Chicago	Hampton Inn Chicago North - Loyola Station	#14 of 197	3.0	4.5
Houston	Comfort Suites Northwest Houston at Beltway 8	#1 of 526	2.5	5.0
	Home2 Suites by Hilton Houston Willowbrook	#3 of 526	2.5	4.5
Philadelphia	Best Western Plus Independence Park Hotel	#3 of 89	2.5	4.5
	Chestnut Hill Hotel	#4 of 89	3.5	4.5

TABLE: Select hotel rankings in June 2018 on TripAdvisor.com

How do these low rated hotels end up in the top spots on TripAdvisor?

This is a two-part answer. The first part is rather obvious with a bit of analysis. The rankings are based on guest reviews, not expert ratings. Even though TripAdvisor keeps their ranking algorithm a secret, we can see that these hotels have earned more 5 out of 5 guest reviews and fewer guest reviews that are 3 out of 5 or lower than their competitors. As you will see when we dig into Prospect Theory, a 5 out of 5 (or "Excellent") guest review means that the guest received far more than she expected for the price paid.

The second part is less obvious and is the more interesting part of the story.

These hotels earned more 5 out of 5 reviews primarily because of the positive relationships, even if they were simply momentary connections that the employees and managers of the hotels created with the guests. We discovered that the language used in the comments at each rating level of online reviews or surveys have specific patterns.

In our extended research of the hospitality industry, we have seen that nearly 90 percent of reviews with a guest rating of 5 out of 5 mention a staff member or manager in a positive light. Usually the descriptive characteristic is modified by a superlative like "very kind" or "extremely helpful." While guests always mention more than one reason for the 5 out of 5 rating, they almost never give that level of review without describing a memory of human connection that created a shared experience.

Why is this significant?

Leaders of a few of the 2.5 to 3.5-star hotels have discovered how to disrupt their market by investing in hiring and training employees who effortlessly connect with guests, rather than in technology, facilities or amenities. They can offer a 5-star experience on a 3-star budget.

Hotels are trying to find ways to compete on experience. Nearly all brands are turning to technology for that solution. They are replacing the human-to-human check-in experience with an app. Some hotels are using robots to vacuum the hallways and deliver food or towels to the rooms. These are entertaining while they are novel, and they may cut costs. They may provide some positive emotion the first few times a guest experiences it, but then, because of the hedonic treadmill, they provide little emotional benefit.

Interestingly, out of the millions of hotel and resort guest reviews we have analyzed in more than ten years of research, we can count on one hand the number of times a guest provided a 5 out of 5 rating and talked about these advancing technologies rather than the people they connected with, when asked, *"Please describe your experience."*

"No matter what function someone fulfills in your organization, they can still contribute to the relationship with your customers."

~Shreesha Ramdas
CEO, serial entrepreneur

Multiple studies carried out by Cornell University and other reputable institutions have proven that when hotels improve their average guest ratings on sites like TripAdvisor, they earn a higher average room rate and increase their occupancy. We have worked directly with hotels and discovered that guests who give 5 out of 5 ratings spend significantly more than guests who give 4 out of 5 ratings during their stay if the hotel offers fee-based amenities and services or has a restaurant. We've also helped hotels raise their rankings on TripAdvisor. In the most successful case where Tony partnered with Kayla (Barrett) Curry, a hotel ranked in the bottom 10 percent of it's market (over 150 competitive properties) successfully improved their guest experience and now hovers around the top 20 percent of hotels in the market and, even here as a 2.5-

star hotel, outranks 4.0-star resorts. This hotel now charges between $50 and $100 more per room per night and has higher occupancy.

Hotels that earn more 5 out of 5 guest reviews earn more revenue due to higher room rates. They earn more revenue outside the room. They attract more guests, which also increases their revenues. It is important to remember this: The one experience guests who give a 5 out of 5 rating consistently report is the positive human-to-human connection they made with employees while at the hotel.

This makes us question the true ROI of technology that replaces people when compared to the ROI of upleveling the social connection skills of employees. It might make sense for a mediocre hotel whose leadership believes they are destined to remain in the middle of the pack to focus on replacing people with technology to lower costs. But, it seems like the message of a false prophet for hotel leaders who want to earn or maintain a top ranking.

Let's look at the PERMA element of Relationship to understand why these connections, even if momentary, have such an impact on the human experience of the guest. To do so, we must understand three things: positivity ratios, kindness boosts, and the biology of love.

Positivity Ratios

Back in the 1970s marriage researchers Dr. John Gottman and Robert Levenson were trying to find a way to predict which relationships would be successful long-term and which ones would not. What they discovered gave them the ability to predict with 90 percent accuracy which relationships would last. They found that, by asking a couple to spend fifteen minutes together attempting to resolve a conflict, it would reveal the one factor that mattered: the ratio of their positive comments to their negative comments. The "magic ratio" for marriages was 5 to 1, meaning for every negative comment, there had to be at least five positive comments. This ratio allowed one person to provide negative feedback to help the other person, but to do so in a framework that immersed the recipient in support and positivity.

Since 1998, multiple studies into positivity have been conducted in the lab, as well as in businesses and schools, to examine the impact of interactions between individuals and teams. While the actual ratios vary for specific segments of the population and the context of the scenario, all of the research agrees that flourishing relationships require more positive than negative interactions. Ratios of about 3 to 1 and up to nearly 6 to 1 are considered essential for a thriving relationship and high performing teams.

In the March 2013 HBR.com article, *The Ideal Praise-to-Criticism Ratio*, Jack Zenger and Joseph Folkman wrote:

"The research, conducted by academic Emily Heaphy and consultant Marcial Losada, examined the effectiveness of 60 strategic-business-unit leadership teams at a large information-processing company. 'Effectiveness' was measured according to financial performance, customer satisfaction ratings, and 360-degree feedback ratings of the team members. The factor that made the greatest difference between the most and least successful teams, Heaphy and Losada found, was the ratio of positive comments ("I agree with that," for instance, or "That's a terrific idea") to negative comments ("I don't agree with you" "We shouldn't even consider doing that") that the participants made to one another. (Negative comments, we should point out, could go as far as sarcastic or disparaging remarks.)"

Our research is not isolated. American Express, in a 2017 study of customer experience, reported *"68% of customers said that a pleasant representative was key to their recent positive service experiences, and 62 percent said that a representative's knowledge or resourcefulness was key."*

Kindness Boosts

"What's the single most mood-lifting thing you can do? It's to go out and help another person. It turns out the way our hedonic system is built, doing something for another person is probably the single biggest boost."

~Martin Seligman
psychologist, educator, author

CEOs and their teams need to understand the power of kindness. Being kind is not just the right thing to do, it creates value for customers that they will gladly pay for. Small moments of kindness, rooted in empathy, help to build bonds between customers and employees that generate returns for the company.

Researcher, Jean Decety identified four distinct processes that take place in the brain that are essential for empathy:

1. Shared affect (mirroring or co-experiencing);
2. Awareness of the other as distinct from self;
3. Mental flexibility to "put ourselves in another person's shoes"
4. Emotional self-regulation to produce an appropriate response

Dr. Paul Zak built on this research by identifying the neurochemistry in our bodies that causes us to do acts of kindness and to build trust. In his book, *The Moral Molecule,* Zak describes how when we share an experience with another person and we are not too stressed regarding our own situation or resources, our body releases oxytocin which is the chemical that helps us feel a bond with another person. We interpret this feeling as empathy and are motivated to take pro-social actions (doing something kind, helpful, or even heroic) for the other person. Our selfless act of kindness inspires the other person to trust us a bit and reward us with an acknowledgement of admiration, gratitude, surprise or awe. When we receive this immediate feedback, two pleasure stimulating neurochemicals are triggered: dopamine which focuses our attention and acts as a reward which reinforces our desire to do this type of kind act in the future; and, serotonin which gives us a mood lift. Being kind is both addictive and feels good.

The effects of this neurochemistry, the brain processes, and the feelings in the body involved with acts of kindness are absolutely essential for CEOs and their teams to understand. Customers who experience these acts tend to have better experiences which leads them to spend more in the current transaction, extend and deepen their relationship with your brand, and promote a positive story about your brand which improves your online and offline reputation and attracts new customers who want a similar experience.

CEOs often wonder how companies like Southwest Airlines or Zappos build a culture of kindness. It is rather simple. First, they hire people who are kind. Then, they encourage these kind people to do more kind things while giving them the authority and resources to act.

In 2011, positivity researcher, Barbara Fredrickson, proved that acts of kindness create a virtuous cycle of growth in people who are already flourishing. By 2013 her thinking on the topic advanced even more when she wrote in her paper, *Updated Thinking on Positivity Ratios*:

"Our results showed that relative to those who do not flourish or who are depressed, people who flourish experience bigger "boosts" in positivity in response to routine daily events such as helping another person, interacting with others, playing, learning, and engaging in spiritual activity. Moreover, flourishers' greater positive emotional reactivity, over time, predicted their growth in resources."

Biology of Love

CEOs who want to disrupt their markets in the next decade need to understand the science of love and how to leverage it in their organizations. The more isolated the advances in technology make humans, the more their primal craving for love and connection will grow. We believe the rush toward the ubiquitous connectivity through the Internet of Things (IoT), the immersion into fictional universes through Augmented Reality and Virtual Reality (AR/VR), and the hyper personalization (as opposed to humanization) enabled by Artificial Intelligence (AI) will create a strategic opportunity for companies to create a whole new realm of human-to-human experiences. These companies will dominate their markets and win not only the current generation of customers, but the next generation who will inevitably recognize the power of human connection because they have grown up with less of it. In other words, CEOs need to see how the value of human connection will grow exponentially because it will be less available in the future as technology replaces humans in more advanced ways every year.

"Ideally, leading with love starts at the top of the organization and is consciously and intentionally woven into the company culture, systems, policies and procedures. We can design love into the way we hire, train, motivate, reward, compensate, discipline, deliver and respond."
~Steve Farber
leadership strategist, author, speaker

Barbara Fredrickson discovered that love is the micro-moment of shared positive resonance between two people. This can be equally applied to personal and professional relationships as it can be between an employee and customer. In her book, *Love 2.0,* Fredrickson explains that through her research she discovered that love, in all its various expressions, comes down to *"the momentary upwelling three tightly interwoven events:*

1. *A sharing of one or more positive emotions between you and another;*
2. *A synchrony between your and the other person's biochemistry and behaviors; and*
3. *A reflected motive to invest in each other's well-being that brings mutual care."*

The sharing, synchrony and mirroring describes a holistic set of processes that happens for every human being. And, we crave it.

Think about the time you really connected with a service agent or a bank teller. Think about the consultant or salesperson who seemed to know you almost immediately. Think about that friend from college or even grade school who you felt an oneness with when you were together.

The hotels we described above that are disrupting their markets and making a fortune doing so are invested in finding, hiring, training and supporting employees who co-create moments of love with their guests. As long as the bed is reasonably comfortable, the room is sufficiently clean, and there are no unpleasant smells, disruptive noises, or unexpected charges on the bill, these hotels will outperform their 4 and 5-star competitors.

Virtually any company can use relationships, as we described in this section, to dominate the growing gap in the market between the companies in their industry that are making massive capital investments to achieve feature and benefit leadership, and the companies led by those who believe mediocrity is their destiny. The challenge some will have with this idea of bringing love into the customer relationship is that is seems too intangible, and they don't understand how to measure it. But, it is measurable if you are, like a prophet, listening to what your customers are telling you they most appreciated about their experience with your company. If the comments in your 5-star reviews, top-rated surveys, executive-level conversations and testimonials refer to the human connection and caring, you are already incorporating love into your customer relationships.

Contemplate Fredrickson's words and consider how creating a culture of love could allow you to dominate your market:

"Love alters the unseen activity within your body and brain in ways that trigger parallel changes within another person's body and brain. More than any other positive emotion then, love belongs not to one person but to pairs or groups of people. **It resides within connections. It extends beyond personal boundaries to characterize the vibe that pulsates between and among people.** [Emphasis added] *It can even energize whole social networks or inspire a crowd to get up and dance."*

M = MEANING

After the global financial meltdown of 2008, homelessness doubled in London. There is one product that can save them: Coffee.

As you read in the Transformation Economy section, one entrepreneur has transformed the coffee industry in London. He observed that Londoners were drinking two cups of coffee a day and that by 2020 the UK coffee industry would need 100,000 skilled employees who were not readily available. That's when Cemal Ezel decided to start a coffee company that hires and trains homeless people to be baristas. The homeless people get a job, a living wage, a bank account, and give back to society by doing meaningful work.

But that's only half the story.

Londoners can now get good coffee and know that they are doing good. With every cup they buy, they know they help someone get off the streets and into safe housing. Every cup they buy makes them a philanthropist, a world transformer. They have the choice to walk down the street indulging in an expensive brand name coffee that boosts their ego and tells the world they can afford to spend a car payment a month to caffeinate themselves, or they can let the world know they are helping solve a problem as old as humanity with every sip.

Change Please is an example of a company that is changing the game in the coffee industry. Their focus is transforming the world. That type of social good can be done in countless ways, but they have tapped into the fourth element of PERMA using a coffee business.

"If we can just get a small proportion of coffee drinkers to simply change where they buy their coffee, we could really change the world,"

~Cemal Ezel
Founder, Change Please

Humans seek meaning in life

Abraham Maslow described his understanding of humanity's search for meaning through his Hierarchy of Needs model. As basic needs like food and shelter are met, we seek higher needs like safety, then love and belonging. Some individuals even reach the level of building their self-esteem and a few attempt to self-actualize or to transcend their conditions and be their best selves.

Seligman points out that in PERMA, meaning includes the desire and pursuit of belonging to and serving something bigger than the self. He teaches people to do exercises where they first think and write about what they want to do to change the world during their lifetime. Then he asks them to imagine it is the end of their lives and they are instructed to write down what their grandchildren see as their most significant contribution to the world. This exercise changes the participants. It focuses them on their most meaningful goals in life. They are more willing to put off temporary happiness and engage in sacrifice in an attempt to help others. They feel and demonstrate more empathy. They feel more fulfillment.

In her book, *The Power of Meaning: Finding Fulfillment in a World Obsessed with Happiness,* Emily Esfahani Smith emphasizes the power and importance of meaning by citing research that correlates the countries with the lowest rates of meaning with the highest rates of suicide.

If you are a typical American, you have probably been touched by the suicide of a loved one, friend or colleague, or you know someone who suffered such a loss. The research shows that "four in ten Americans have not discovered a satisfying life purpose." A disturbingly high number of youth in America lack a sense of meaning.

Consider the research on employee engagement. Gallup shares in *State of the American Workplace* report that in 2015 - 2016, 51 percent of American workers were disengaged (employees are psychologically not attached to their work) and 16 percent are actively disengaged (resentful that their needs aren't being met and are acting out their unhappiness). Employees cannot reach a state of engagement or flow because they do not have clear, meaningful goals to pursue.

Meaning is not one-dimensional. Smith writes, *"When people explain what makes their lives meaningful, they describe connecting to and bonding with other people in positive ways. They discuss finding something worthwhile to do with their time. They mention creating narratives that help them understand themselves and the world. They talk about mystical experiences of self-loss."* The four pillars of meaning Smith analyzes in her book are:

- Belonging
- Purpose
- Storytelling
- Transcendence

Let's take a take a look at each.

Belonging

"At a time when we are more connected digitally than ever before, rates of social isolation are rising. About 20 percent of people consider loneliness a 'major source of unhappiness in their lives' and one third of Americans 45 and older say they are lonely."

~Emily Esfahani Smith
writer on the human experience

While leading the development and implementation of an award-winning Voice of the Customer program for a large financial services company, Tony had the opportunity to have conversations with the contact center representatives. One evening, a representative told him that, about every two weeks, he receives a call from an elderly woman who was a lifelong customer. She would call him and ask one or two simple questions that took all of a minute or two to answer, but the conversation would often last 30 to 45 minutes.

The representative went on to explain, *"She is a widow. She called me a few years ago after her husband of several decades died. I worked with her for a few hours over a two-week span to get her accounts straightened out. The week after we finished she called back. She was overcome with sadness and loneliness because she missed her husband. She told me she had no one else to call. So, I sat there and talked with her for like 45 minutes. Whenever she said, 'Oh, I am wasting your time,' I replied, 'I can talk with you all day if you like. My job is to take care of customers. You've been our customer for life."*

According the General Social Survey, Americans have virtually stopped discussing important matters with other people. In

1985 researchers found that the most popular response to their question about how many people they shared important matters with, was three people. By 2004 the most popular answer had dropped to zero. Loneliness is on the rise even while people are more connected than ever before. People who feel lonely also report their lives as being less meaningful and rates of suicide in these populations are higher.

Smith's research led her to conclude, *"Close relationships and high quality connections have an important feature in common: both require us to focus on others."* She went on to say, *"Compassion lies at the center of the pillar of belonging. When we open our hearts to others and approach them with love and kindness, we enable both those around us and ourselves—and the ripples of our compassionate acts persist, even long after we're gone."*

Starbucks prophesied the need for a third place (i.e. home, work, Starbucks) as people stopped gathering in community centers, churches and temples. They responded by building the coffee shops where people would come to connect, share and bond. According to Statista, Starbucks had over 27,000 locations worldwide in 2017.

Facebook launched in 2004 with a similar prophecy. People would want to gather and connect online, even with strangers from across the globe. By June 30, 2017 the company reported that there were over 2 billion monthly active users.

The faster technology advances and people disconnect from human-to-human interactions, the more value companies will find in creating moments of belonging, easing the pain of loneliness and providing safe and enjoyable ways to connect and reconnect with people who are "like us" and those who are very different.

Betsy had the opportunity to see the concept of belonging play out at the executive level in a way that took all those who witnessed it by surprise.

It's customary when recruiting members to a Customer Advisory Board to ask them to commit for a term of 12, 18 or 24 months, with the idea that by rolling people on and off the board, historical conversations are not lost while new ideas are incorporated as additional members are added.

On one particular board in which Betsy was involved, there was a brilliant man who was somewhat curmudgeony and had a rather tough outer shell. He was a very vocal member of the board, and had a demeanor that sometimes made it appear that he would rather be anywhere else.

When it was time for him to roll off the board, he was presented with a beautiful engraved plaque and was honored in front of his peers for his service on the board. No one could have predicted the emotion that then flowed out of his every pore. He said he didn't want to roll off the board and had been dreading this moment for quite some time. He went on to say that he had developed such a bond with the other members of the board, as well as the team from the host company, and that no longer belonging to this group felt like a death he was grieving.

Everyone in the room felt that display of emotion, with several other members of the board echoing the sentiment expressed by this gentleman. Imagine the feelings of the host company, knowing that they had created an environment that resulted in this level of commitment, belonging, loyalty and meaning for some of their most valuable customers.

Purpose

CEOs, with their rolling three to five year vision can understand how purpose can bring meaning. Stanford psychologist William Damon says purpose has two dimensions: First, it is a "stable and far-reaching" goal we continually pursue which we use to organize our decisions and motivate our behaviors. Second, it involves a personal contribution to the world. Extrapolate the effects a purpose has on a company and you can see why companies that succeed usually have a clear purpose. It provides a framework for organizational decision-making and behaviors. It focuses the team on more than just the mundane daily tasks by giving them a "why" that explains their struggle. They see their work as a way to help others. Companies that succeed in the future will find ways to create that same sense of meaning for customers so they can be certain that their purchases are helping others.

Storytelling

"Stories are particularly essential when it comes to defining our identity—understanding who we are and how we got that way. We have a primal desire to impose order on disorder—to find the signal in the noise."

~Emily Esfahani Smith
writer on the human experience

Storytelling is an essential part of customer experiences. It helps customers bring coherence to their experiences so they can make sense of their decisions, behaviors and outcomes. Whether it is told across the office cubicle wall, written on

Yelp, or posted as a live video on Facebook or Snapchat, customers tell stories. CEOs may call these stories surveys, reviews, focus groups, client advisory boards, customer conversations, emails, video chat sessions or by any other number of names. If the customer is explaining what they need, why they need it, what went wrong, or what they expect, it is likely that they are telling a story. And, if they are telling you a story, they are sharing with you what is meaningful and why it matters to them.

Stories have heroes and villains. While analyzing online customers reviews, Tony recognized a fundamental pattern. 5-star (Excellent) reviews consist of the customer telling a story that makes the company or the employees the hero because they helped the customer experience multiple elements of PERMA. However, 1-star (Terrible) reviews are usually stories where the company or employee is a villain who created a problem and did not make restitution, while the customer takes on the heroic role of being an avenger who rights the wrong by doing all they can to hurt the company's sales; or, the customer becomes a protector of the innocent by warning others to avoid the trap they fell into. This storytelling gives the customer a sense of control again.

Remember the complexity of emotions? The dimension that motivates action is feeling dominance or an internal locus of control. This is a key reason why people post negative reviews. They are trying to regain control of the chaos they are experiencing by making sense out of it with a story that makes the company the villain.

Much like Change Please does, companies can find ways to strategically and tactically help the customer become the hero of their own meaningful story. This involves the customer realizing that they transformed in a way they hoped for and you promised was possible as a result of using your product, service or experiences.

Transcendence

"The most beautiful thing we can experience is the mysterious. It is the source of all true art and all science. He to whom this emotion is a stranger, who can no longer pause to wonder and stand rapt in awe, is as good as dead: his eyes are closed."

~ Albert Einstein
theoretical physicist, developer of the Theory of Relativity

When we are faced with a mystery, something we cannot explain because we cannot comprehend it, we are left without words in a state of awe. You've probably felt this when walking on the beach by the ocean, in a forest or maybe at the edge of the Grand Canyon. This is the state of transcendence.

David Yaden of the University of Pennsylvania, studies the state of transcendence. His research indicates that two things happen to trigger awe, the emotional response to mystery. We no longer have a sense of self or anything related to the ego like concerns and desires. It is replaced with a deep connection with others and even an oneness with the world or the divine. Peace and well being wash over us.

In the face of mystery, our worldview is shaken. We don't have the mental models to comprehend what our senses perceive. We lack the words to communicate what we are witnessing and experiencing. This causes our brains to have to do a form of a reboot followed by an upgrade where we install new mental models that give us the ability to find the words and to begin to understand the world and our place in it in a whole new way. Researchers Michelle Shiota, Dacher Keltner and Amanda

Mossman published the first scientific studies of how awe affects our sense of self in 2007.

"We feel awe when we perceive something so grand and vast that we cannot comprehend it, like a magnificent vista, an exquisite piece of music, an act of extraordinary generosity, or the divine."

~Emily Esfahani Smith
Writer on human experience

Awe has been identified as one of four emotions of the Admiration Equation™ that customers express when they have a 5-star experience. It is a such a powerful emotion that it can be confusing to experience. Smith writes about the phenomenon, *"This is the paradox of transcendence. It simultaneously makes individuals feel insignificant and yet connected to something massive and meaningful."*

Some companies are better able to inspire awe than others, but every CEO should consider their options and the prophets must be listening to the customers to hear what creates awe. Performance companies like Cirque du Soleil rely on awe as a way to create viral word-of-mouth marketing. Restaurants with views of the skyline or ocean have location advantages. Large resorts like those in the Gaylord Hotels portfolio that have acres of gardens under an atrium of glass surrounded by hundreds of guest rooms leave guests speechless. Even product packaging and presentation can inspire awe. Steve Jobs and Apple mastered the art and science of triggering moments of transcendence when people first open their iPhone or MacBook boxes. These moments are described by customers in their stories as they strive to make sense out of what they witnessed and reconstruct their worldview from their new perspective.

Transformational companies like Change Please are now integrating their entire business model, product and service development, and customer engagement around this concept of meaning. They don't just tack something on as if meaning is additive. The good cause or the moments of meaning and the work of the business are inseparable. CEOs and their teams must find ways to create a sense for their customers that belonging to a community while pursuing a purpose changes the world. This requires that they wrap the company's purpose in a story that motivates people to be part of the transformation the company is leading. It involves sharing customer stories to keep the meaning fresh and vibrantly alive. They must do this all while helping people transcend their own conditions to realize they can be, do and have more than they imagined.

A = ACCOMPLISHMENT

"I did it the hard way. I did it with the shin splints and the burning lungs and the boredom and the 'what am I doing out here?' feelings."

~Josh Clark
creator of C25K

According to an article on Nokia.com's health blog, when Josh Clark, creator of Couch to 5K (C25K), started running back in 1996, he did not do it for the love of running. In fact, it took weeks of pain, boredom and doubts to finally reach a breakthrough point where he felt the rewards of running:

spikes in creativity, the runner's high from endorphins, and feeling better in general. Clark was glad he made it through the first few weeks without giving up, but he knew that many others would not work through those unpleasant experiences to achieve their goals. Giving up was more logical and the body would confirm that it was the only decision that made sense.

Clark realized that, like so many things people attempt to do in life and business, failure is inevitable on the path toward success. So, he set out to identify smaller goals that would reward the person working toward them if they did just a bit more today than yesterday. C25K helps people who have no regular exercise routine be prepared for a 5K in just 9 weeks. According to site c25kfree.com, over 5 million people have used the system. The reason for the success is that the promise and expectation of a new level of achievement triggers the desire system in the brain to override logic, pain and doubts to motivate the new runner to get up and go for their goal yet again.

"Accomplishment (or achievement) is often pursued for its own sake, even when it brings no positive emotion, no meaning, and nothing in the way of positive relationships." - Martin Seligman

Successful CEOs can likely identify with this desire to win, or to master something, simply for the sake of doing it. Most of them are driven by the desire to achieve. Some people find the reward of achievement in just doing the task through the pain that comes with mistakes, failure and restarting again and again. Researchers Anat Keinan and Ran Kivetz discovered that some people have an "experiential resume" that they accumulate experiences on or a bucket list that they check experiences off as they have them. They are pursued for the sake of the list, not necessarily for the sake of the positive emotions, engagement, relationships or meaning. In other words, achievement alone is sought.

Behavioral economist Dan Ariely and Michael I. Norton coined the term "conceptual consumption" in their 2009 research. They reported that consumers make illogical decisions to change consumption patterns of physical products based on their preference for certain concepts. As an example, one may choose to buy an SUV, not because they have a need for the size or space or the need to go off-road, but rather because they identify with the lifestyle the SUV represents.

Another form of conceptual consumption involves the pursuit of badges in apps or on membership sites. Judd Antin and Elizabeth F. Churchill researched this pursuit through gamification and reported five different reasons people pursue badges. In their paper, *Badges in Social Media: A Social Psychological Perspective*, they wrote, *"We deconstruct badges and present five social psychological functions for badges in social media contexts: goal setting, instruction, reputation, status/affirmation, and group identification."*

CEOs must carefully consider whether they would build more loyalty through the triggering of positive emotions that are measured in some form of customer satisfaction survey, or if their customer base (or specific segments of it) would be far more loyal if the company developed and delivered of an achievement system. This latter approach requires an understanding of how top performers push themselves to work through the challenges that they will face in the uncertain pursuit of success. In fact, providing guidance for the next step toward success and then reporting on the evidence of forward progress tied with the recognition of effort are the foundations for any achievement system.

Grit researcher Angela Duckworth has analyzed thousands of cases of accomplishment versus failure. She created a formula that is highly relevant for CEOs and their teams to be aware of.

Talent X Effort = Skill

Skill X Effort = Accomplishment

The key with this formula is that one can be born with talent, but effort is far more important for accomplishment. The unpleasant experiences and emotions that accompany the effort build grit.

With effort being the key to success, we can look to the work of Carol Dweck. In her research in schools and in businesses, she found that those who realized their potential successfully developed because of their "growth mindset," whereas those who did not reach their potential were plagued by a "fixed mindset." When a person believes they can learn new skills that they have not yet mastered, they adopt and act from the growth mindset. Those who believe their skills are set and cannot be improved demonstrate a fixed mindset.

CEOs who can step back to see how this matters to their own success, their team's success and their customers' success will be able to dominate their market. Consider this: Your customers must believe they can grow their skills (growth mindset). They must put in the effort especially when it is hard and results are not evident (grit). They need to believe there is a path and have confidence in the exact next step (goal setting). They need to be praised for their efforts and small wins on the way to the major achievement (gamification). In all of this, their behavior will change (conceptual consumption).

If you would like to download resources to help you apply PERMA in your business, go to
www.ProphetAbilityBook.com.

SUMMARY

The elements of PERMA are from the human experience perspective. It's interesting to think about how this applies to an organization in a B2B setting. For all the differences one can point to between B2B and B2C, the most significant element of both is that humans are the purpose and the providers of any business. So ask yourself, *"What is the human experience of the CEO or CMO or Customer Success agent or a mid-level manager? Which of these elements, or combination of elements, really drive them as human beings, as individuals and as professionals in their company?"*

Perhaps the user of the software wants to feel positive emotion, engagement and relationship, so they actively participate in software that has been gamified. Maybe a customer service agent desires a relationship with the customer they are trying to serve, so they require quick access to information so they can be extraordinarily helpful to the person on the other end of the phone. In essence, because of what the human being wants to experience, it will drive their behavior and how much they like or dislike the product or service you provide.

CHAPTER 3
HUMAN EXPERIENCE IN BUSINESS

SELF CONCEPT IN BUYER BEHAVIOR

As long as 40 years ago, it was recognized that self-concept and self-identity impacts buyer behavior. An article in Business Horizons in October of 1977 said this:

"Purchase motivation is a function of the image a person wants to convey to others about himself. As self-concept changes over time, what changes can be expected in buyer behavior?"

While in the B2B space we say we are doing business with other businesses, but as we previously illustrated, no business is out there making a purchase; rather, individuals are making the purchase, so influencing the individual is really the key because they are the ones ultimately making the buying decision.

Purchase motivation is a function of how the person sees themselves. A CMO who is buying a marketing technology or a consulting engagement is being influenced by their self-concept. They will ask:

- Who am I?
- Who do I want to be?
- Can I be the hero that transforms this company?
- Can I achieve something no one else here has ever achieved before?

What they are considering is who they want to be, what they want to do, what problems they have and what they want to do about those problems.

There are actually two levels to be aware of if you are doing business with another business:

1. *"Who do I want to be as the person in this B2B transaction?"* If you're selling to a person in another business, you need to consider their self-identity.
2. *"What is it that influences the identity of this company? Where do they want to go?"* This is where the CEO's vision comes into play and where they see their engagement with the company long-term.

Some 40 years later in 2016, Savita Hanspal and P. Raj Devasagayam published, *Impact of Consumer Self-Image and Demographics on Preference for Healthy Labeled Food,* which contained new research on self-concept. On the surface, this may seem like a strictly B2C topic. But consider this example:

A restaurant is a B2C business. However, there are a lot of B2B suppliers to the restaurant. This illustrates the B2B2C concept. Grocery stores and technology companies are other examples of B2B2C. The point being, the B2B companies that are in the B2B2C space are ultimately influenced by the consumers and what the consumers want, thus healthy labeling is an example of that.

Hanspal and Devasagayam open their paper with this quote: *"Self concept or image consists of the totality of thoughts and feelings having reference to him/herself as an object. It's composed of the attitudes one holds toward oneself."*

As you go throughout your day in different contexts, you are a different person. You have different self-identities depending upon the circumstances. You see yourself as being someone different. Most often, you are not aware of who you are being in a particular moment. It's only upon reflection that you see that you were a different person. We don't have just one identity but rather many, many identities:

- I am a wife/husband.
- I am a mother/father.
- I am a daughter/son.
- I am a sister/brother.
- I am a friend.
- I am a business owner/CEO.

But even within those, there are more identities. They are basically four parts to the individual self-concept:

- **Real self concept**
  - The self-concept that's driving me in that moment. Who am I now?
- **Ideal self concept**
  - I would like to transform to become this person. Who would I like to be?
- **Social self concept**
  - The perception I have of what others think about me. How do others see me?
- **Ideal social self concept**
  - I would like to leave this impression. How do I want others to see me?

These all influence how we purchase. We may make purchases because of who we want to be and because we want people to see us a particular way. Or, we may make purchases because of how we see ourselves or because we think people see us in a particular way.

Here's a B2C example from a customer's review of a lawnmower found on the Home Depot website.

"After 24 years of great service from my Honda, it was time to retire that old mower. I was going to buy a new Honda mower, but when I was at Home Depot, I saw the EGO mower. I have always been suspect of electric mowers not having enough torque or battery life. So I pulled out my phone, read some of the reviews here and watched a couple of YouTube videos. In addition, a friend of mine just bought one and she had rave reviews. I bought one, still suspect of its capabilities. Well, I just mowed my lawn (1/4 acre) for the first time this year and I am very pleased with my EGO lawn mower...It's light, quiet, and no more dealing with gas and oil. The one handle deck height adjustment is a nice feature."

This customer describes his process of transforming from a being a loyal Honda lawn mower customer and electric mower skeptic to the point of being a fan of the EGO electric lawn mower. He becomes such an advocate for the product that he shares his enthusiasm in this review. His self-identity changed while shopping, evaluating and using the mower. Each of these transformations was required for him to be ready and willing to take the next step.

Our research shows that when people are contemplating a purchase, it's actually subconsciously happening weeks or months in advance and the structure of their language in response to the questions we ask can reveal exactly what they want to purchase, when they are ready to purchase and what they ultimately will purchase.

We are seeing this more and more. What's happening is their subconscious is dealing with the conflict between their real self, ideal self, social self and ideal social self. Only after this gets worked out does the customer become consciously aware of it. As a result of going through the psychological processes of grappling with who a person believes themselves to be, and finding the coherent story to tell themselves, they adopt a new self image, change as an individual and change their purchasing patterns.The statement above holds true for B2C and B2B.

SHOULD HAVE SEEN THIS COMING
Epi-Pen: A Preventable Failure

I (Tony) invested in my first EpiPen after nearly dying in a hotel room as you previously read. I made the decision to never travel without one after my first experience with anaphylactic shock. I remember watching my girls, who were 3 and 5 years old at the time, sleeping across the room, peacefully unaware that I was moments away from death. I did not want to lose time with them, and I did not want them to lose me.

Since then, the EpiPen has given me a new sense of calm and the freedom to eat out with caution, but not worry. It has given me the freedom to travel and have dinner with clients or at conferences, without being embarrassed that I am so picky about my foods. In fact, the EpiPen marketing made others aware of the challenges those of us with allergies have and how serious it can be.

Mylan, the maker of EpiPen experienced what so many of our clients have been afraid of facing—a negative viral campaign in the media and on social media.

I rely on EpiPen like over three million other Americans. I carry the medication with me because it stops a life-threatening reaction to certain foods. And, like many others, I was concerned about the sudden and drastic price increase in 2016.

I confess, I do not understand all of the workings of pricing in the pharma industry and am not qualified to comment on the decision in a rational way. Instead, I will help you learn from

Mylan's decisions so your business may be able to avoid a similar negative viral campaign.

Mylan's decision to raise the price of EpiPen falls in line with the rise in U.S. drug prices. Fortune reported that between 2009 and 2012 generic drug prices increased by 8 percent per year. Reuters reported that four of the top ten most widely used drugs in the U.S. had price increases of over 100 percent since 2011. Another report shows that Mylan's EpiPen price increase is dwarfed by another decision the company made for a 542 percent increase in ursodiol, a generic medicine used to treat gallstones.

Looking at the EpiPen Strategy

If you track the story back just a bit, you'll find that Bloomberg ran an article sharing the background strategy that led to the growth of EpiPen from a $200 million product in 2007 to a $1 billion product that delivers about $1 of epinephrine per dose. EpiPen had margins of 8 percent in 2008, but those skyrocketed to 55 percent in 2014 and accounted for 40 percent of Mylan's operating revenue. This particular part of the story is fascinating.

Heather Bresch, Mylan's CEO, realized that she could market the drug to the parents of children with allergies because there was a deep connection to be made with the fear of loss these parents live with daily. She then lobbied to have the drugs available in schools and the public buildings similar to defibrillators because of the life-threatening condition many allergies pose. This marketing strategy was coupled with gradual price increases. It was only recently that they did a triple-digit price increase. This is where she made her mistake and why this particular decision went viral and generated so much negative press.

How the EpiPen Strategy Backfired

Bresch saw that the drug could play on the fear parents have of their children facing life-threatening allergic reactions without medical treatment being readily available. And, that fear is a massive motivator. The problem was that after the price increase, the fear worked against Mylan and Bresch.

EpiPen, like so many other products, is really a type of insurance against a relatively unlikely event. I suggest that this is an example of conceptual consumption. Products that serve the role of insurance are really far more useful when they are owned because they provide peace of mind and are seldom used. Think about the number of ways you insure yourself from loss. You probably have car and home or renter's insurance. You likely have life insurance for those who survive you. And, you definitely have health insurance.

Did you also think about:
The Insurance . . .
- you bought with your newest technology device
- you pay to the electric or water company to cover damage between their lines and your home
- you have on your loans if you lose your job
- included in your furniture, lease or car payments

Buying . . .
- the bulk package of toilet paper so you don't inconveniently run out
- snacks in case you get hungry between meals
- cold or flu symptom medicine in case you feel under the weather

The point is this: We buy many things for the sake of feeling like we will still be in control if life doesn't go as we planned. And, this is what Mylan and Bresch relied on to increase the sales of the EpiPen. The EpiPen gave parents and their kids dominance again. It made them able to live a bit more freely, with a bit less worry of being caught without life-saving medical treatment. Freedom. That is what we all want.

Where Mylan Went Wrong

Based upon the research we've done with clients who have products that provide a feeling of 'insurance from uncertainty,' it seems that there were three things that converged to cause the negative viral reaction.

1. The triple-digit price increase. We've seen it happen repeatedly with products that have an 'insurance' feel to them. People react very negatively when there is an instant triple digit increase in the actual dollar amount or when there is a series of smaller increases of double digit percentages over several years. But this alone is not enough.

As I shared above, EpiPen was making increases and had more than doubled in price over the last several years. And, there was no outrage when Bloomberg referenced Mylan's marketing approach. In fact, the video interview seemed to convey a bit of admiration and the gradual increase was used as a contra-example to the other drug price increases that were taking national attention at the time.

2. Explanations are too complex. This is the second key to the EpiPen virality. I believe the company could have been able to continue the gradual growth for some time, but when they initiated the triple-digit price increase, it triggered the attention of people. Then, when consumers and advocates asked why, there was no simple explanation that made sense to the public. Worse yet, there is no explanation that makes sense to a parent who knows her child may need the EpiPen or face death. This brings in the third element that makes this such a viral story.

3. Valence-Arousal-Dominance (VAD). As shared above, emotions have many characteristics. In our customer experience analysis consulting, we look closely at the valence, or the level of positivity or negativity of the emotion. However, the arousal and dominance factors of an emotion are key to things going viral.

The anger and outrage parents expressed are high arousal emotions. They are coupled with the fear of loss (of a child and/or of the access to freedom and safety that EpiPen's presence provides). Where fear alone can be a low dominance or submissive emotion, it seems to shift to a high-dominance emotion when we feel like something is being taken from us (see Prospect Theory). This likely triggers a sudden dose of testosterone and a rich cocktail of emotional chemicals that move us to attack the threat aggressively.

WHY WE'RE IRRATIONAL

Prospect Theory

"People think about life in terms of changes, not levels. They can be changes from the status quo or changes from what was expected, but whatever form they take, it is changes that make us happy or miserable."

~Richard Thaler
Nobel Memorial Prize in Economic Sciences
Author of *MisBehaving*

Daniel Kahneman and Amos Tversky, two Israeli psychologists, questioned the old economic theories of the rational human and the concept that we always make the best choices because we are reasonable beings. As a result of their research, they developed what is known as Prospect Theory.

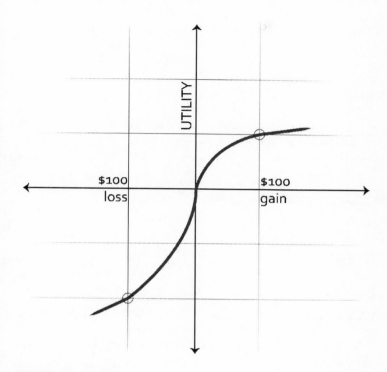

CHART: Prospect Theory

On the chart above, you will notice two intersecting lines. The horizontal line represents your financial losses or gains while the vertical line (utility) basically refers to your level of happiness with an event.

As you can see, the curve that goes up and to the right means that the more you gain, the happier you are. Makes sense. Also notice the curve that goes down and to the left. That means that the more you lose, the less happy you are. Again, makes total sense. You may also see that both curves diminish the further they go. This is because we feel the relative change more intensely at first.

Where the two lines intersect is your status quo or your expectation. In other words, if in a transaction you receive exactly what you expect, you will not experience a loss or gain and you will not be more or less happy than you are before that transaction.

When you look at the curved line, one thing becomes clear. People like gains but they hate losses more. This is called loss aversion. The drop in the curve to the bottom left is far steeper than the curve representing the gains.

Consider this example

Imagine one of us hands you a $100 bill. You probably feel a bit surprised and delighted by our random act of kindness. You can feel a definite shift in your emotion.

What are you going to do with this $100 bill? Will you use it for something you wanted to buy for yourself? Will you use it to buy a gift for another person? Will you give a portion of it as a donation? Just thinking about the possibilities may be pleasurable.

Now imagine we take the $100 bill back from you. This is also likely to generate an emotional response but it would be an unpleasant surprise. It might even start you moving downward into an emotional spiral that feeds your thoughts like, *"I can't believe they did that,"* or even, *"I knew it was too good to be true."*

This is notable because it was just an imaginary $100 bill, yet this exercise can create a real shift in emotion that is palpable. When we do this thought experiment from the stage at conferences, both the person who receives the imaginary money and those who observe the experiment often report feeling worse after the money is taken away than how they felt before we started the experiment. In reality, your financial status did not change at all before, during or after the experiment, yet you may have negative emotions associated with the experience.

When Kahneman and Tversky performed this exercise with real people and real money as part of their research, they discovered that people feel the pain of losses roughly two times more intensely than they feel the delight of the gain. In other words, if they unexpectedly lose $100, they would have to receive $200 unexpectedly to return to their emotional status quo. Getting just the $100 that was lost back is just not good enough to return them back to their original level of emotion.

What's also fascinating is that there is a diminishing emotional impact the more one gains or loses. In other words, the more we gain, the less we feel the relative pleasant impact it has and the more we lose, the less we feel the relative unpleasant impact.

To understand this, imagine that someone gives you $10. You will feel a boost of positive emotion. By contrast, you will feel a surge of negative emotion if someone takes $10 from you. But if someone gives you $100 and then a moment later gives you an added $10, the incremental $10 will not feel as good as the $10 you received in the first experiment because you are judging it against the $100 you just received and it is small in comparison. It will be far less emotionally impactful.

$0 + $10 compared to $100 + $10

The same holds true with regard to losing the $10.

As Richard Thaler's quote above points out, we only notice the change. Life experience is about the change we feel rather than the objective reality. Think about waiting in a line. It may not actually be a long wait, but it may feel like a long time passes before you receive service, and the way you feel is relative to the thing you are judging it against. That could be your expectation of how long the three people in front of you will take to be served. It could be the speed of the lines to your left or right. It could be the speed this company or another company has taken in the past to serve you. Value is determined by change from the reference point, which is the status quo or one's expectations.

The relative change from your status quo or expectation determines how much you feel a gain or a loss.

Prospect Theory Applied to Customer Experience

In the chart below, you will see how the Prospect Theory applies to customer experience in both B2C and B2B business.

We adapted the chart created by Kahneman and Tversky to be relevant to what you might find in online reviews or on an internal survey with ratings being expressed on the curve as Terrible, Poor, Average, Very Good and Excellent. The vertical line represents the level of happiness or the emotional value of the experience. The horizontal line represents the perceived financial outcomes (gain or loss).

Using the five-point scale, you can see the relative perspective. The "average" rating equates to a customer having their expected experience or receiving the status quo in the industry for the price they paid. The customer may be thinking, *"This is what you promised and that's what I got."* Customers typically do not provide a 5-star rating for receiving the experience that they asked for and expected to receive. Customers who are unfamiliar with your company, products or experiences may reference their expectations of your industry to establish their expectations. Remember, they need something as a baseline to create their expectations of the experience before it happens.

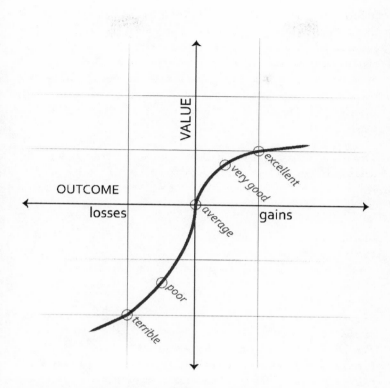

CHART: Prospect Theory Applied to Customer Experience

When someone provides an above average rating, it means that they received a better than expected experience for the price. If the rating is below average, the customer received a worse than expected experience for the price they would normally pay. Keep in mind, that the pain of loss is approximately two times more intense than the pleasure of gains, which is why angry customers seem to be irrational. They deeply desire resolution, recompense and closure.

When you are a leader in an organization and wonder why some customers are just being jerks, it's important to remember that the reason they are angry is because they are feeling pain from a loss. And, humans want to avoid loss because it is hard-wired as a survival tactic. If a loss happens, you have to empathize and try to figure out not only how to cover their losses, but how to go above and beyond by several multiples, maybe surprising them in a positive way, to get them back to a minimum of their expectation if not to exceed their expectations.

On the flip side, gains create a "positive conflict" in the customer's mental accounting, so they then feel the need to reciprocate. They may want to spend more in the moment, provide a recommendation, pay more in the future, bring people along with them next time, etc. Have you ever decided to stay for dessert after a great meal because you wanted to extend an amazing experience a bit longer, or have you tipped your server more than you customarily would because they were so good?

The reason you don't see a lot of 3-star reviews or average ratings in surveys is because customers don't have a lot of emotion attached to your company meeting their expectations. It's only when there is emotion, either positive or negative, that people feel compelled to discuss their experience. In fact, it is only when they feel a sense of dominance (they are in control or want to take control back) that they will write a review or share a story. If you were neither that great nor that bad, they will have nothing to say that will help others, to boost their reputation or social capital, or to reciprocate for a terrible or excellent experience. They got what they expected so why would they talk about you?

A Very UpLyfting Story: Loss + 2x = Raving Fan

I (Betsy) had just arrived at the San Francisco airport to attend a 2-day Customer Success conference. Although I was not new to ride-sharing, I had yet to figure out all the ins and outs of various airports with regard to how they treat Lyft and Uber riders.

I had put in a call for a Lyft driver and was waiting for him outside baggage claim near a door labeled "Ground Transportation." It made sense to me that this is where my driver would pick me up. However, I was mistaken. After getting an alert that my driver had arrived and not seeing him, I called his mobile to ask where he was. It was then he told me that due to specific airport requirements, I had to go upstairs to meet him. I asked him to wait, he agreed, and I told him I would be there within 30 seconds, which I was. When I arrived upstairs, I got a notice that the driver had cancelled the ride, and then I was dinged with a $5 "No Show" charge. Not only did I have to start all over with the process and let the person I was to meet with know that I would be running late, I had five dollars automatically charged to my credit card. I felt pain and I felt loss.

After the conference, I emailed Lyft and told them of my experience and respectfully let them know how unhappy I was. I provided screenshots that I had available to me through their app, and I politely asked for my money back.

A mere six, yes six minutes later, I received the following email from Lyft:

Hi Betsy,

Thank you for reaching out.

I'm sorry to hear about this, we're always happy to help in any way we can.

After reviewing the details of your ride request, it appears that this situation did not warrant a cancellation fee. We've gone ahead and refunded the $5 fee, which will post to your account within 3-5 business days.

As it relates to your experience with the driver, for security reasons, we are not able to reveal what actions might be taken; however, I can let you know that we take our passengers' complaints very seriously.

As a courtesy, I have applied a credit to your account that will give you $5 off a Lyft ride...

Thanks for your valued feedback. We are always looking for ways to improve our services to create memorable experiences for our community members.

Best,
Geovanni

Not only did I receive my original $5 back, but I received an additional $5 credit within six minutes of issuing the complaint. Now think what that did to my mental accounting. I immediately posted about my experience on LinkedIn which, in very short order, received 26 likes, 7 comments and 2,236 views. Do you think that might have been worth more to them than the $5?

The coincidence is not lost on me that I had this experience with Lyft while going to and from a Customer Success conference.

HEROIC STORYTELLING

"Personal stories and gossip make up 65% of our conversations."

~Jeremy Hsu
journalist

In 2011 an antiquities smuggler and the Sulaymaniyah Museum in Slemani in Iraq, struck a backroom deal for $800 which would change how we read one of the world's oldest stories. While inspecting the mud-caked clay tablets covered in cuneiform writing that the smuggler brought to the museum, Professor Farouk Al-Rawi of the School of Oriental and African Studies (SOAS) at the University of London spotted one tablet of particular interest. He believed the tablet to be about 2,600 years old and advised the museum to purchase the tablet for negotiated price.

While examining the piece, Al-Rawi suspected the tablet contained previously unknown verses of the 4,000-year story, The Epic of Gilgamesh. With the help of Andrew George, associate dean of languages and culture at SOAS, Al-Rawi was able to translate the ancient writing in five days. They discovered twenty new lines of the famous poem that were alluded to elsewhere in the previously translated text, but were missing from every other version of the story.

LiveScience.com reported that the tablet, *"tells the story of Gilgamesh, king of Uruk, and Enkidu (the wild man created by the gods to keep Gilgamesh in line) as they travel to the Cedar Forest (home of the gods) to defeat the ogre Humbaba."* The rich description of the sounds and life of the Cedar Forest are a revelation. More significant is the insight the text provides into the internal emotional conflict the heroes feel after killing the ogre and destroying the forest. They suspect that their act of destruction of nature will anger the gods.

Humanity has been telling stories long before we developed written language. The discovery of the new verses of The Epic of Gilgamesh shows that that the structure of stories and the emotions expressed are not a new development. But this story from the tablet found in Iraq is young by comparison to the oral traditions researchers working with documented accounts from ancient Aboriginal tribes in Australia have uncovered. According to an article on ScientificAmerican.com, they found geographic evidence that stories recounting the rise of the oceans when ice caps melted over 10,000 years ago have been passed down as oral tradition accurately for over 400 generations. These examples demonstrate that humans are wired to tell stories to help us remember what is important and the lessons that are valuable to us as individuals and groups.

Why Customers Tell Stories

Why do stories matter in a book about why businesses succeed, fail and bounce back? Because as Jeremy Hsu pointed out, *"personal stories and gossip make up 65% of our conversations."* Many of these personal stories that we tell include our interpretation of our experiences as a customer. In our economy, we spend 24 hours a day as consumers.

Think about it this way: Your home, car, food, electricity, water, cell phone and service, lawn care, bed, clothes, air conditioning, education, the computer you use at the office, and probably everything else you use daily was purchased by you from someone else. This means, in today's world—unlike any other time in human history—your human experience is essentially an integration of customer experiences resulting from your engagement with a wide variety of companies, brands, products and services. This means that most of the stories we tell today inevitably involve at least some of our experiences as a customer.

We've invested over twenty years studying the stories customers tell in surveys, online reviews, social media posts, videos, interviews, focus groups, customer advisory boards, emails, and on phone calls. Through all of that research we've realized that the stories customers tell of their experiences fulfill essentially the same purposes that any other story they tell does. According to researchers, stories help us:

1. Make sense of our lives, decisions and transformations
2. Persuade ourselves and to know who to blame or give credit to
3. Discover our identities of the past, present and future

Dan McAdams, PhD, a Northwestern University psychology professor says, *"When people turn episodes from their lives into anecdotes, it's not just to entertain friends. Stories allow us to make sense out of otherwise puzzling or random events."*

The events of your life may seem puzzling or random for a number of reasons; however, two in particular merit our attention: 1) Your senses have limitations and cannot detect everything around you; and, 2) Your conscious awareness cannot process all the data that comes into your subconscious mind from your body. Yet, you are wired to rationalize the events and experiences your conscious mind is aware of. You must make sense of the events in your life or your mind will discard them.

Let's look at these points more closely. Your bodily senses have a limited range of detection. You can only hear a small number of the sound frequencies that exist. You can only see a sliver of the light spectrum present all around you. While you can smell and taste, your abilities to detect and distinguish flavors and scents are far more limited than a dog's. Each cell and the systems within your body can detect your bodily needs, but these are also limited. You may be hungry, but you don't know what you are hungry for. You may feel tired, but you aren't sure if you need a nap, some caffeine or a quick jog around the block to be refreshed. Even with these limitations, your body is sending millions of bits of data to your brain that are processed in your subconscious mind every second.

Researchers still dispute exactly how much data is sent to the brain. Regardless of the exact amount, they all agree that the processing power and bandwidth of the subconscious mind is exponentially greater than the conscious mind. Some say there is a 200,000,000 to 1 ratio of data processed in the subconscious versus conscious mind. That means that, out of all of the limited data your senses can detect and subsequently send to your brain, only a tiny fraction of that information ever gets to the conscious mind where you actually are aware of it. Research supports the theory that the reticular activating system (RAS) contributes to the subconscious to conscious filtering process. The process is better addressed at length elsewhere. We only mention it here to make you aware of it and to pique your interest in it.

When you grasp how limited your body is as a user interface to the world around you—face it, no UX designer would settle for a product that has the deficits humans have—you can begin to appreciate why you need to tell stories to yourself and others. Stories help you piece together the many siloed data streams from your senses so you can make sense out of your snapshot experiences.

"Stories help us smooth out some of the decisions we have made and create something that is meaningful and sensible out of the chaos of our lives."

~Dan McAdams, Ph.D.
professor, department chair, Northwestern University

Stories of struggle can give us hope. Stories of turmoil can help us grow wiser. Stories of failure can convince us we're incapable or not worthy of success. Stories of bounce back can inspire us. We use stories to persuade ourselves to believe what we want to believe about ourselves. But we don't stop there. We tell stories about others so we can persuade ourselves to believe who is to blame for our misfortunes or who we ought to give credit to for our successes. We choose to ignore what is not useful to or does not fit into our stories.

John Holmes, PhD, a psychology professor at Waterloo University says, "For better or worse, stories are a very powerful source of self-persuasion, and they are highly internally consistent. Evidence that doesn't fit the story is going to be left behind."

When we persuade ourselves through stories to believe something about ourselves, it can transform how we behave and who we become. The stories we tell ourselves help us build our identity of the present and transform how we identify ourselves in the past or in the future. McAdams found in his research that people who told stories of meaningful events in their lives using a "redemption sequence" (bad events have good outcomes) compared to those who used a "contamination sequence" (good events have bad outcomes) changed their identity and their behavior. They believed they had a responsibility to improve their communities, to teach others what they learned, and they were ultimately happier. McAdams wrote in *Personality and Social Psychology Bulletin* (Vol 27, No. 4), *"Having a redemptive story behind you gives you the confidence, or at least the hope, that your work will bear fruit in the long run." (Personality and Social Psychology Bulletin (Vol. 27, No. 4)*

Jonathan Adler, Ph.D., a psychology professor at the Franklin W. Olin College of Engineering, shared in Psychotherapy Research *(Vol. 18, No. 6)* that when psychotherapy patients tell coherent stories where they are the central figure of the story, it is a significant predictor of future improvement. In another (unpublished) longitudinal research study, he found that patients felt better after telling stories about themselves taking control in their lives again.

Stories shape our identity and future behaviors because they change how we remember events as well as our role and the roles of others in those events. If we begin to assign fault to characters in a story, even months later after we have forgotten the story, we will still remember who is to blame. *"Stories shape memory so dramatically,"* says Holmes. *"Once you tell a story, it's hard to get out of that story's framework, and they tend to get more dramatic over time."*

Holmes adds, "Storytelling isn't just how we construct our identities, stories are our identities." This is why storytelling, in the context of customer experiences, matters so much. As customers, we become what we tell ourselves and others about our experiences.

STRUCTURES OF STORIES

There are many templates for storytelling, and we find as far back as Aristotle that there were recommended structures. A common one is the three-act story.

- Act 1: Define the quest of an unwilling hero
- Act 2: Engage in internal and external conflict
- Act 3: Achieve resolution and transformation

Pixar, the animated feature film company that Steve Jobs purchased after being kicked out of Apple in the mid 1980's, has their own version of a successful story structure.

- Once upon a time there was _____. (an unlikely hero)
- Every day _____. (a glimpse into the hero's life and his desire to be, do or have more)
- One day _____. (an event that changes everything and incites a decision by the hero)
- Because of that _____. (a chain cause-effect events that result from the decision)
- Because of that _____. (the continuation of the chain of cause-effect events)
- Until finally _____. (something irreversible happens the transforms the hero and the world around him)

When most business books or articles dive into storytelling, they are usually focused on how companies should use the concept in their marketing. Google the term "storytelling in marketing" and you'll receive nearly 1.3 million results. Look at the articles written on the topic and you will notice that the number of articles explodes in early 2015 and has continued to be a major topic of interest for marketers. If you analyze Google Trends, you can see that the search term gained traction in late 2011 and has steadily grown in use since 2013.

While storytelling may be an important tool for marketers to communicate their messages to consumers, that is not our focus in this book. We are taking a very different perspective, and we suggest you might find it valuable should you choose to do the same.

The most important story is not what your company says to your customers, but rather what your customers say about you to themselves, to their family, friends and followers, to strangers, and to you.

The stories customers tell matter more than your own marketing because customers don't trust your marketing. 83 percent of customers don't trust ads according to Nielsen. Havas Media reported that only 22 percent of consumers trusted brands. Couple this with the data that shows word-of-mouth marketing and consumer generated content like online reviews are the most influential factors in prospect decision making and you have a compelling argument for paying close attention to the stories your customers are telling everyone.

While the next section of the book will dive deep into why to listen, what to listen for, and how to listen, the remainder of this chapter will share what we have discovered about the structure of customer stories. To reiterate a point we made earlier, we recommend that you view your customers' comments in surveys, online reviews, social media posts, emails, calls to your customer service center, chat sessions, focus groups, customer advisory boards and conversations over coffee with a friend all as stories.

Every customer story has a hero and a villain. While analyzing online customers reviews and survey comments, Tony recognized a fundamental pattern. Top rated reviews and surveys (5 out of 5 for online reviews) consist of the customers telling stories in which they are transformed and receive more than they hoped for or desired because of the admirable, awesome or gratitude-inspiring actions of the employees.

However, in 1-star reviews customers share stories where the company or employee is a villain who created a problem that they then did too little or nothing to resolve. In these stories the customers take on the heroic role of being an avenger. They publicly attack the company to embarrass its leaders, burnish it reputation, and hurt sales. In doing so they feel they are giving the company what it deserves—a form of reciprocation through revenge-—to right the wrongs committed by the employees or leaders. Some customers choose the role of protector of the innocent, rather than being an avenger, so they sound a warning to help prospects avoid the trap they fell into. Whichever path the customer takes in the 1-star review, they are the hero and the company transforms into a villain.

This latter form of heroic storytelling gives the customer a sense of control over their lives and their experiences again. It helps them make sense out of events that caused them to feel confused, frustrated or angry. The stories transform them from victim to victor. They are attempts to return to their state of normalcy where there is order and balance is restored.

Most customer service or customer experience professionals pay far more attention to the stories in negative reviews and low rated surveys. Too few ever consider the value of the comments that accompany a top rating. And this is where the real return on investment is. Prophets must analyze what happy customers are saying as much or more than what unhappy customers are saying so they can identify patterns that are unfolding and which will lead to future success for the company.

THE ADMIRATION EQUATION

Storytelling structures have been around for millennia, but only in recent history have customers had the ability to tell their stories to thousands of strangers in a way that has a direct financial impact on the company the story is about. The rise of TripAdvisor, Facebook, Yelp, Google My Business, Angie's List and countless other sites gave customers a structured way to review businesses.

Tony's work with customer reviews led to a discovery about the structure of 5-star (Excellent) reviews and top-rated survey comments (if the survey asks questions in a particular way). What he discovered is now referred to as the Admiration Equation because it is a formula that companies can use to engineer 5-star experiences. We share it here because it will help the prophets in your company understand how to read the stories your customers are telling the world. Once they know how to read these stories, they will be able to foresee where their company's strategy for products, services and experiences must inevitably go, and they have a roadmap to get there.

There are the five factors of the Admiration Equation. The first three revolve around the storytelling your customers are doing, and the last two help you deliver excellent service consistently so you can maintain the 5-star experience that the first three factors earned you.

Creating the 5-star experience requires:
1. Multiple Micro-Moments
2. Multi-Sensory Micro-Moments
3. Positive Micro-Moments

Maintaining the 5-star experience requires:
4. No Unexpected Negative Micro-Moments
5. No Unresolved Negative Micro-Moments

Let's dig into each of these factors in more detail so you can understand each and see how they all work as a system to transform your customer.

1. Multiple Micro-moments

Three or more micro-moments, which last no more than a few seconds each, within the context of the 'experience', are essential. Experiences are constructed in the mind of the customer, so you need several micro-moments that are remembered. These will be used as the key points in their story and frame how they see your brand, products, service and experiences. These multiple micro-moment experiences are required for transformation.

What is a micro-moment? Psychologists define a moment as about three seconds long. Anything less than that is a micro-moment. We mentioned micro-moments in relation to Barbara Fredrickson's research into to the biology of love. She demonstrates that micro-moments of resonance between two people are what make us feel love.

In Malcolm Gladwell's book, *Blink*, he talks about what happens in the fraction of a second to about two seconds when an expert is looking at a piece of art, or a police officer has to make a decision before their rational thinking can kick in. What do they decide? These decisions take less than a moment. He, too, is talking about micro-moments.

It is in these micro-moments that your customer determines how they feel about your brand, product, service or experiences, and they decide what they will think. You don't have to have a perfect customer journey to create a 5-star experience. You do have to be absolutely certain that you get the moments that customers remember absolutely correct.

We make decisions between three and seven seconds before our rational brain processes that we made the decision. We then rationalize the decision or try to change it. There is a delay because the emotional brain operates much faster than the rational brain. In these moments when our emotions are triggered, our reason can be hijacked for either pain or pleasure.

No matter how long the event is, whether a few minutes (a transaction at the cash register) or days long (a conference you attend for your business), there are three to five micro-moments that get mentioned, and those micro-moments become the context for and structure of the story your customers will tell from that day forward.

2. Multi-Sensory Micro-Moments

These micro-moments must simultaneously engage a variety of emotions or senses with internal and external stimuli. They capture the attention and focus it pre-consciously. The experience feels immersive.

The multiple micro-moments must engage a variety of senses at exactly the same time through both internal and external stimuli. It's not just what connects one with the outside world through their senses of taste, sight, hearing, etc. that matters to your customer. It's also what connects them with their internal world. Do they feel fulfilled? Do they feel like they saved money? Do they feel like it was a good deal? Do they feel more confident now than before? Do they feel like they were part of something special? Consider all of the ways they could experience the five elements of PERMA.

This goes way beyond a traditional example of a customer experience. The experience actually feels immersive. It's like jumping into a swimming pool. The experience takes over the customer's perception of reality. It takes control of their mind. They become convinced that it is reality.

Soon it will be commonplace to have virtual reality and augmented reality in our daily lives. These technologies will be as common as the cell phone is today. We will have experiences that we project into our brains through our senses using devices designed to fool us into thinking we are in a new universe.

This is not unlike a 5-star experience. When you have a 5-star experience, whether B2B or B2C, you are involved in an alternate, augmented or virtual reality at that moment in time. You are transported from the life of the reality that you are living into a brand new space. Read customer stories and you will see how they escaped their reality and took on a whole new one for a short period of time. More importantly, look at how that alternate reality helps them transform and adopt a new identity that they keep living from after the event and the experience is over. This is what transformative experiences do.

3. Positive Micro-Moments

Once our preconscious attention is captured, we construct positive, often high-arousal emotions that then guide our rational thought when it finally engages. As we saw in a previous chapter, the PERMA model represents the positive experiences that are sought.

As our preconscious attention is captured, multiple senses and emotions are triggering, and we aren't even aware of it yet. We begin to construct positive, high-arousal emotions that make us feel like our whole body is engaged. High arousal simply means we are aware of emotions like anger, frustration, joy, happiness, excitement, surprise, thrill, admiration or awe because the create a measurable and noticeable physiological response. They hijack and guide our rational thought.

What are positive micro-moments? Again, think back to the PERMA model. They are positive emotions, engagement, relationships, meaning, and achievement. You may experience these factors of PERMA in any number of ways. For example, achievement might include feelings of confidence, fulfillment, and empowerment.

If you look at your 5-star reviews and your top surveys from customers who are absolutely thrilled with their experiences, you will find that they are telling stories with multiple, multi-sensory, positive micro-moments.

4. No Unexpected Negative Micro-Moments

Negative surprises are often interpreted as threats or danger. This results in the construction of negative emotions. Informing the customer in advance of possible negative micro-moments can be beneficial.

Unexpected negative or unpleasant micro-moments are perceived as threats or danger. These perceptions cause your customer to construct negative emotions, like fear, which captures their attention. As we saw in Prospect Theory, when customers feel as if they are going to lose something, it feels at least twice as bad as the positive of an equivalent gain. Negative emotions get our attention faster, deeper, longer, more intensely. As a matter of fact, there are more negative emotion words in the English language than there are positive ones by several multiples.

If you know there will be some unpleasant, negative micro-moments, it behooves you to inform your customers in advance. You can potentially create meaning from it as well.

For example, let's assume you join a CrossFit gym, right on the heels of making your New Year's resolution to start working out regularly. You get there and are all fired up to crush it. And although you expect to be sore and tired soon after your workout, and possibly the next day or two, no one advises you that you are going to be really sore for possibly for a week or so afterwards. You may not know that it's going to be really hard to get out of bed for multiple days in a row. This will create a negative experience that may keep you from going back for quite some time.

It would be far better if the trainer would say, *"Hey, you haven't exercised in a while. CrossFit is different and we are going to build you up over time. But because your body's not used to this, you're going to be in some pain tomorrow. Maybe tonight, but definitely tomorrow. You just have to keep moving and I promise, you will feel better. And honestly, this may happen every time you work out for the first week or so. It's going to feel bad and you're not going to want to come back. I'm telling you this so you know that when you push through that, probably some time in Week 2, you will quit feeling so much pain and actually feel more vibrant and alive. The endorphins will be more prominent than the pain."*

If they were to tell you that up front, you would be appreciate their honesty but probably wouldn't think much of it at the time. When you wake up in pain every day for the next week, you will remember what you were told and realize that it's normal rather than a negative experience. The pain has been given new meaning.

This is just a simple example of how you can use your new understanding of PERMA to differentiate your company from the competition without investing a dime in new features or benefits. Simply providing the information you know at the right time within the right context can shift you from being a villain to being a hero and make your customer a loyal advocate.

5. No Unresolved Negative Micro-Moments

Customers need harmony and psychological closure. Even when a customer is previously informed of a potential negative micro-moment, they need resolution.

Even if a customer is told of a potential negative micro-moment like we just saw in the Cross-Fit example, they also need to be told of a possible resolution.

"Here's what to do before you go to bed tonight after today's workout. If you wake up sore in the morning, which you probably will, do A, B, and C."

A customer must be prepared to deal with an issue they know is going to happen. It's not enough to just tell them it will happen. Psychologically, they will need a resolution.

This also holds true if something unexpected happens (i.e. a torn muscle). Otherwise, it will not be a positive experience for the customer. It is rare indeed to see a high score on a survey or a 5-star review with an unexpected negative micro-moment, much less a negative micro-moment that was unresolved. Your customers must know what they are facing and must know the way to resolve it.

APPLYING THE ADMIRATION EQUATION

If you are asking yourself, "Why are we looking backward at what our customers said in reviews and on surveys when this book is about ProphetAbility?" The answer is simple.

We've consistently found that the more we study what customers are saying in these particular channels where we can see a self-reported rating, the more we learn about who they want to become and how they want to transform in the future. This is what a prophet needs to understand so they can help the CEO see three to five years into the future.

Consider what you learned about Prospect Theory as applied to customer experiences. Customers give average ratings for the experience they expect to have today. They give below average ratings for the experiences that are below their current expectations. And, they joyfully give 5-star ratings for those experiences that exceed their expectations and often even their hopes. In short, today's 5-star reviews contain clues about what your customers are going to expect and give average ratings for in the future.

Do you remember dial-up Internet access? We were thrilled just to be able to connect and see what was online. What do you suppose customers wrote as comments in top-rated surveys back then? Probably how happy they were with their speeds. And, eventually we got faster and faster speeds. We were thrilled again, and what might we have stated in our top-rated surveys then? Probably that we were so happy that we now had enough speed to connect two or more computers with a splitter. And, speeds continued to rise and modem manufacturers expanded the number of ports so we could attach even more computers.

We could go on. The point is this: What customers admire you for today will be their expectation and the industry norm in the future. If you want to disrupt your competition, you have to stop being so concerned about what you're not doing right (that which is mentioned in low rated reviews). Just fix these problems and move on. Invest most of your resources in imagining and then creating the new versions of the transformative experiences that customers already admire your brand for.

Once your team masters listening to your customers through online reviews and surveys, they will be able to listen to your customers through other channels such as email, phone calls, chat sessions, in-person conversations, or Customer Advisory Boards, and be able to immediately identify if a customer is telling a story that is a 5-star experience or not. We've trained analysts, managers, executives, even front desk agents, nurses, doctors, and others what to listen for after we discovered (through reviews and surveys) what a 5-star experience sounded like for each of their companies.

The Patterns in Customer Stories

The comments of each rating level of surveys or reviews have specific patterns of language. The Admiration Equation outlines the five factors that create and maintain a 5-star experience. The language in the comments of these top rated reviews reflect:

- Admiration of skill
- Admiration of goodness
- Awe
- Gratitude
- Superlatives with positives (very kind)
- Connection with staff
- Transformative experience

You may not see all of these in a 5-star review, but you will see some of them in every 5-star review. The first four are what psychologists call "outward facing emotions." These are unique in that you only see them in the highest level of a survey or a 5-star review. They are also different than other emotions because the customer is actually feeling them about someone else rather than about themselves. Each of them triggers a unique reciprocal action.

For example, if you admire the mastery of a skill someone has acquired, you are more likely to go attempt mastering a skill yourself. If you admire the goodness of another person, you are more inclined to go do acts of kindness or moral goodness for others. If you are in a state of awe, you'll likely want to go do something that makes you feel like you are part of something bigger than yourself and is in someway meaningful to others. And if you are filled with gratitude, you will want to go give to someone else or return the favor. These outward facing emotions move you to transform and be a better person.

Conversely, if you look at emotions like joy or excitement, they are not outward-facing emotions. Customer happiness is just joy within themselves, whereas when the Admiration Equation is applied, customers become outward facing and do good in the world because they have experienced a transformative moment with your company. It keeps that ripple effect going beyond themselves. Different companies have different ways of creating these transformational experiences. All of them master the consistent excellent delivery of some combination of the elements of PERMA.

When you look further down the Prospect Theory curve at 3-star reviews or average survey results, you will see language like:

- It was a fair trade
- Got what I paid for
- Some good, some bad
- A focus on the features or benefits

At this level, customers clearly have a different experience. They stop talking about connecting with individuals and focus on describing the features and benefits they used. There are various expressions of fairness or equity. In some cases, there is a form of mental accounting that happens where they describe what was good or great and what was bad or terrible. They balance the accounts to essentially determine that they paid an appropriate price.

Often times we find that customers will tell others that it might be worth the experience, but they will not return again. Customers who get what they expect have no reason to reciprocate. You will not have loyal customers if you simply provide what they expect. You must know what matters to them and be consistently excellent in those areas. Your three to five year plan must be a roadmap that develops the core competencies that continue to create consistent excellence in the areas revealed as admirable in top-rated reviews.

When you study comments in 1-star reviews, you find language that is much harsher, including comments and demeanor such as:
- I've been robbed!
- ALL CAPS ARE USED
- Rude, disrespectful staff
- Critical failure of features
- Staff not helpful after repeated attempts to resolve
- Expected benefits were missing

Usually the comments that accompany the lowest ratings show the customer is in pain and suffering even as they remember the experience. Some are hateful in their expressions.

Remember that loss aversion drives people to feel losses far more intensely and longer than they feel an equivalent gain. What's also particularly harmful to your brand at this level is that mentions of your team are usually extremely negative. Instead of connection, there is a sense of isolation and helplessness. Stories emerge of how rude and disrespectful or unhelpful the team was.

If the customer experienced the failure of a feature or a benefit they were expecting was not delivered upon, it could shape the entire experience. In fact, a single negative unexpected micro-moment could trigger a downward emotional spiral that hijacks the customer's brain and limits their ability to see anything good. Their reticular activating system will filter the sensory input and only allow in the threats and dangers, so they see the world differently.

Again, we want to remind you, with proper training, you can "listen" to the language used in emails, chat conversations, phone calls and Customer Advisory Boards to accurately predict what kind of rating or survey response the customer would provide. You can glean whether the experience was excellent, average or terrible. In a reactive mode you can then trigger a set of actions the team can take to resolve the issue for this particular customer at this particular moment. Strategically, you can leverage the listening skills of your entire team to identify what your customers uniquely admire about your brand, products, services and experiences right now so you can build your vision for the future.

This holds true in both B2B and B2C. Below are real reviews from McDonalds as an example of a B2C company. See how many of the traits of each level of review you can identify using the lists above. Then look to the B2B examples from Gainsight reviews. Below we provide a quick analysis of Gainsight and some commentary to consider.

B2C Example

Real World Examples from reviews of McDonalds on TripAdvisor.com

5-star Review: February 2016
Nice
"Kayla Was very nice and sweet I just adore her and the rest of the staff food is always hot and ready"

3-star Review: November 2017
Average
"Slow service. had to wait for staff to have an argument with a customer. Did not eat in. bad vibes after watching the argument"

1-star Review: January 2018
Broken Ice Cream Machine
"In true McDonald's fashion, their ice cream machine was broken. Stopped for an ice cream and machine was broken."

B2B Example

Real World Examples from reviews of Gainsight on Appexchange.Salesforce.com

5-star Review: July 2017
AWESOME product and people
"I have worked with Gainsight at 2 organizations and have had a fantastic experience both with the product and the staff. Gainsight has allowed our teams to have better visibility into their accounts and prioritize who to engage with. It has also helped standardize the CS onboarding process as you can create specific CTAs and playbooks for your various teams. The people are top notch! From implementation to support to

our CS and PS teams that have helped us, they are each knowledgeable while also being willing to take a step back and fully understand the situation to determine the recommended approach. I highly recommend!"

3-star Review: February 2016
Hopefully it will be great
"I think this tool can and will be great, but it does have some work to get there. The good news is they release regular updates and seem to listen to what their customers want/need and work them into their roadmap.

1-star Review: March 2015
Pricing on website? Nope. Nowhere. So, going to GetSurveys.com.
"In this day and age when people have transparent pricing on survey technologies that integrate with Salesforce.com (47 others) and don't buy during business hours, you should put your pricing / packages on your website. Simply because of this I went to getsurveys.com. What are you trying to hide if you believe in the price and efficacy of your product? Shady."

A Quick Analysis of Gainsight's Reviews

Gainsight is a B2B company that offers a software product designed to help organizations rally their entire company around retention, expansion and customer success.

In the 5-star review above, you can hear how the customer's company was transformed by the use of the Gainsight product. *"Gainsight has allowed our teams to have better visibility into their accounts and prioritize who to engage with."*

They also talked about the people who helped them transform. *"The people are top notch . . ."*

We had to go back to 2016 to find a 3-star review, meaning that Gainsight is doing some amazing things, actually living what they help other companies do: create customer success. Most ratings are 4- and 5-star reviews.

In this review, it's clear to see that it was early on in Gainsight's history. The reviewer did note that there were some good things, but that there was more to do. You can see that they don't feel cheated because they see the company is constantly working to improve based on customer feedback.

And finally, going all the way back to 2015, we found the one and only 1-star review. The reviewer complained that the pricing was not available on their website, indicating that they were looking for transparency. However, since Gainsight offers custom software, it would be impossible to post pricing on their site.

Additionally, it appears as if this reviewer was actually looking for survey software, so she may not have been the right customer for Gainsight. This is an important point. Are your lower reviews from the customers and prospects you are trying to attract? That's not to dismiss it, mind you, but rather a strategic question to ask. *"Have we positioned ourselves correctly, or are we attracting the wrong customers through our marketing who we are not here to satisfy and transform anyway?*

This is why the CEO can't just be aware that there is a CX or Voice of the Customer program. The CEO must be involved. The CEO must have the information because he is the one who says, *"This is who we are as a company. This is the vision of where we are headed. This is who we serve."* The CEO has to strategically dictate the positioning of the company. Marketing carries it out but the CEO has to make the decision. CEOs have to have access to unfiltered information so they can make the right decisions as to who their customers are and who they are not.

Just because a company receives a bad review, doesn't mean it did something wrong. The company may have done the right thing but for the wrong customer. This is very important to keep in mind. Sometimes the marketing messaging is not in alignment with what the company is there to deliver. Once this is realigned, the company sells more, retains their customers longer and receives more and more positive reviews.

The following is a blog post by Gainsight CEO, Nick Mehta, which was posted immediately following a Gainsight-produced conference in 2018 that drove more than 5200 attendees to two days of professional education around the concept of "Customer Success."

We include this post, not as an endorsement of Gainsight, but rather to illustrate how thinking about the human experience should come from the top. As we discussed previously, it's important for organizations to understand the purpose . . . the why . . . and Nick is able to articulate it in one succinct sentence:

"To be living proof that you can win in business by being human-first."

This powerful post reflects many aspects of the human experience (remember the PERMA model) as it relates to business, including that of the leader, the employees, and the customers.

THE BRIEF MOMENTS IN TIME

By Nick Mehta, CEO of Gainsight
Reprinted with permission.

Sad fact: Some of the most profound moments of my life have happened on United Airlines red eye flights.

While I may have a love-hate (or rather hate-hate) relationship with the incessant yet "unexpected" flight delays, increasingly tiny legroom in Economy "Plus," and "No-Go" in-flight WiFi, the sheer exhaustion of overnight flights forces my brain into a contemplative state. And I've done a ton of red eyes. I don't count because the number would be too brutal, but it's definitely several hundred.

As I'm leaning on the cold window of seat 9F trying to sleep, I end up in a recurring loop of thoughts:

- **Envy** and anxiety about the friend's company that just got bought for a ton of money, or about the college classmate who seems to be "killing it."
- **Longing** to have been at the school event for my kids and to trade FaceTime for the real thing.
- **Wonder** at the billions of stars that beckon from the window of my window seat.

I only know myself really… but I like to think—or perhaps hope—in a shared-pain-sort-of-way that we all have those moments: the WTF-AM-I-DOING-WITH-MY-LIFE moments. The IS-IT-ALL-WORTH-IT refrains in the cacophony of the day.

And some of this brings me back to earlier moments in my life:

My dad showing me the cover of Time Magazine in 1984 with Bill Gates on it as a wunderkind…

A famous VC telling me after my first two startups failed that I better *"watch out or people will think you're a **serial failure...**"*

The feeling of pride after selling my last company and regret for what more it could have become if we went for it a little bit longer...

As the leader of a company, I think about this issue in both the first person singular (what am I doing?) as well as the first person plural (what are we doing?). I feel a responsibility to perhaps not answer the question, but at least ask it on behalf of many others: What's the point of it all?

Welcome to the Matrix

As with all of life, nothing that I'm saying is new. Scores of Harvard Business Review articles and Cliffnote-friendly business books have articulated the importance of defining a "Purpose" for a company.

And yet... so much of business can feel aimless and empty. For sure, they tell us to focus on the bottom line—or the top line—or some line, I guess. It's all about shareholder value. Pray to Adam Smith every night and your company's soul will be redeemed the morning you ring the bell on Wall Street.

Companies certainly have gotten smarter. They know how to talk the talk. They hire the consultants and do the offsites. The values are written in really nice fonts in really pretty colors in really expensive frames. The purpose statement or mission statement or vision statement is stated with marketing flair.

And yet... so many people work at so many companies and don't believe any of it. They are cynical about work—and for good reasons. They've had their hearts broken. Speeches unfulfilled. Promises unmet.

Employees are told to act "businesslike" at work. Emotions should be left at the door—unless that emotion is greed. The biggest barrier to your success is your feelings. Act with more poise. Show more gravitas. Don't let them see you sweat. Show any sign of vulnerability and people will pounce on it. The only thing that matters is the company. It's a dog-eat-dog world out there—no room for little puppies. And seriously, it's not personal—it's just business.

Sometimes it feels like Shakespeare was writing about the corporate world in Macbeth:

"It is a tale, told by an idiot, full of sound and fury, Signifying nothing."

Don't get me wrong; some leaders are the embodiment of Purpose. When you're trying to save humanity by flying rockets and cars into space to one day colonize new worlds, it's maybe alright for feelings to take a back seat.

But if your first name isn't Elon, how do you find meaning in it all? If your job, like mine, is doing something that you think is important but isn't quite in the category of "the future of human existence," how do you justify it to yourself and your team? Enterprise software can certainly be a good business, but can it feel good too?

Lost In My Mind

I guess I'm doomed to dwell on this a lot because my real heroes aren't in the business world at all: Plato. Socrates. Descartes. Newton. Godel. Marie Curie. Einstein. Heisenberg. Vera Rubin. Planck. And now Hawking. The scientists and thinkers whose whole lives were a quest for meaning.

In case you don't know, while by day I may roam the world preaching Customer Success and SaaS best practices, my nighttime mind wanders—reading about quantum mechanics, philosophy, metaphysics, consciousness, and the meaning of reality and time.

My heroes lived lives that, for me, were full of Purpose. Heck, in Einstein's *Annus Mirabilis* year of 1905, he wrote three of the most important papers in scientific history in just 12 months. At 22 years old, Newton invented what went on to become Calculus. Hawking's life was so meaningful that it doesn't seem poetic or coincidental he was born on the 300th anniversary of the death of Galileo and died on Einstein's birthday, it's somehow just "right."

And when I look up at the stars, as I do pretty much every clear night, my role in this grand show seems like I'm barely an extra. Maybe we all feel that way sometimes?

Finding My Way

But recently, a lightbulb went off for me. I've always believed in the concept of Servant Leadership at work—where the managers are there to serve their teams, as opposed to driving them.

At Gainsight, we've always—from day one—been extremely values-driven as a company. And our values are a bit… quirky:

- **Success for All:** Our "bottom line" requires us to drive success for not only shareholders, but also customers, teammates, their families, and our communities around us.
- **Golden Rule:** Treat people the way you'd like to be treated.
- **Shoshin:** Cultivate a "Beginner's Mind."
- **Stay Thirsty, My Friends:** Have ambition that comes from within.
- **Childlike Joy:** Bring the kid in you to work every day

So it hit me

We may not change the world with what we do, in a realistic sense. But we can change the worlds of those around us in terms of Why and How we do the things we do.

At Gainsight, we long for something different in the Why and the How of business. We respect the bottom line and recognize its importance, but we don't bow down to it as our only master. People are just as important as business—and they aren't "assets," as some companies might claim. Not everything has to drive to shareholder value, because you can have multiple goals. Teammates can thrive at work without having to give themselves up in the process.

In fact, we believe society needs this more than ever. With Artificial Intelligence, Automation, Robots, and the like, homosapiens are having our own existential crisis. Every screen, selfie, and social network makes us long that much more for a real smile and shared moment.

Our Purpose

So we finally wrote it down. We decided on the Why that would keep us going long beyond the day-to-day. And that Why is:

"To be living proof that you can win in business by being human-first."

"Human-first" means always thinking about people in the decisions you make about business:

- Human-first means realizing that the life and time of the person running your office and that of the person cleaning your office are equally important and valuable.

- Human-first means being radically transparent with your team—even when it feels uncomfortable.
- Human-first means making sure that the company's schedule and work/collaboration environment are flexible so your team can make the piano recital, friends' night out, or family trip.
- Human-first means welcoming every teammate like they are the most important person in the company—because they are!
- Human-first means congratulating and celebrating a teammate that is leaving for their next dream job versus treating them like a traitor or trying to make them feel guilty.
- Human-first means thinking about your competition not as evil or bad, but rather as a bunch of people just as good as us trying to live their lives and support their families.
- Human-first means leadership, including CEOs, opening up to their teams and to the world about their brightest dreams and their darkest fears.

Does human-first mean you don't make tough decisions? Of course not. Human-first companies will do things from time-to-time that don't feel great. But my test for myself is if I'm causing pain for others in the interest of a "rational" decision, I better be feeling that pain myself many times over—or I've lost my humanity. That pain is what will make us always think of people in decision making.

At Gainsight, we feel like we can help a lot of humans—between our customers, our teammates, their families, our shareholders, and our communities. Maybe it's not all of humanity, but it's a start.

And if we, like many other companies going down this path, can help other businesses open their eyes to another way to work, that impact can grow even more.

In short, for us, it's not business—it's personal.

And in a recursive sort of way, I think our Purpose nests well in the Purpose of the Customer Success Movement. Customer Success is fundamentally about realizing that your customer is not a transaction or a deal or an opportunity or a lead. Your customer is a bunch of human beings just like you. And just like you, they want to succeed with what they do.

In a way, Customer Success is about bringing humanity back into this technology-driven world.

In Closing

One of my favorite vacation activities is to stare at the ocean. I can do it for hours. Something about waves just feels magical. And yet, when you think about it, waves are nothing more than water being pulled by energy (from the moon, mostly).

And like waves, companies are nothing more than the people inside them, motivated by energy. And if we all do it right, our people—and our companies—will be unstoppable.

Einstein said it well:

"Not everything that can be counted counts, and not everything that counts can be counted."

Here's to the things that truly count in business.

CHAPTER 4
LISTEN TO THE GODS

INTRODUCTION TO UNFILTERED LISTENING

As you read in the beginning of this book, when Lou Gerstner was hired at IBM, he was essentially promoted from customer to CEO. He leveraged his experience as a customer to turn the company around. He traveled to Europe to meet his team and to meet with and hear directly from clients. He had dinner with CIOs who were among IBM's customers, and then he spoke to their colleagues about how he was bringing the customer back to the center of IBM's focus. He directed his top fifty leaders to meet with clients and report back in writing what they heard and made it clear that they also needed to direct their leaders to do the same. Because of his weakness as a technologist, he leaned on his tremendous capacity for listening to the unfiltered messages of his customers. This is how he guided IBM successfully through its bounce back.

Unfiltered listening is more important today when humanity is creating more data and information each year than in all of humanity's history. There is so much data, that we can easily get lost in capturing it all, analyzing it all, and determining what it all means. This is a recipe for failure.

There is often a disconnect between the information CEOs need and the information they receive. With every member of the C-suite needing different information to make decisions on how they will run their day-to-day activities while planning for the next quarter or year, the CEOs need something more. They are responsible for deciding the future three to five years of the company, but using the data from this week, last month or last quarter. This is like driving a car by looking into the rearview mirror. If the CEO cannot see through the windshield to the horizon, the company is doomed.

This is where unfiltered listening comes in.

Just like when you drive a car, your head needs to be on a swivel checking your blind spots, monitoring oncoming traffic, and looking for the signals and signs ahead. As the CEO, you need to be looking at multiple sources of information. Most of that information exists outside of your company.

You need to be considering the disruptors coming up alongside of you in your blind spots. You need to consider the shifts competitors and regulators are making as they come at you. You need to be watching for signals and signs of changes in your customer's desires, needs and aspirations. This is why CEOs and their teams need to understand PERMA. Every human is seeking a combination of those five elements of well being and happiness, and competitors will disrupt you by finding new ways to fulfill those desires.

Like Lou Gerstner, you cannot rely only on those in your organization to give you the unfiltered information. You need to hear directly from the people who are the experts: your customers, vendors and competitors.

In this section we are going to describe unfiltered listening and give examples. We will explain what unfiltered listening is not, as much as we will share what it is, because to do it well, you must understand both.

UNFILTERED LISTENING

Yesterday's prophets listened to their gods after they altered their conscious state by engaging in rituals or using mind-altering substances, including inhaling fumes from a hole in the earth. Some of these ancient prophets had direct access to the king and could share what they heard. In other cases, between the prophet and the king there were many administrators, managers and generals who interpreted, modified or stopped the prophecy before it reached the king. They did this because they:

- Misunderstood the prophecy
- Were threatened by the prophecy
- Were trying to protect the prophet or others
- Saw an opportunity to advance their agenda
- Didn't believe the prophecy
- Feared the king's reaction to the prophecy

Prophets today face these same challenges. They seldom have direct access to the CEO and their message, if it makes it, may be modified by those who pass it up through the organization. We refer to this interpreting, modifying or stopping of the prophecy as filtering. It is not making the message better, but rather, it is an attempt to remove some unwanted element of the message or to prevent an unwanted outcome.

Filtering can happen subconsciously or unintentionally. Remember playing the game of telephone when you were a child? One person would start by whispering a message into the ear of another. Then, one by one, each recipient turned and whispered what they thought they heard into the ear of another person. The last child would tell the whole group the message they received. Maybe you laughed or furrowed your brow trying to figure out how what you said to your partner ultimately turned into what the last child said.

Despite, or maybe because, we have the ability to communicate with anyone at nearly anytime today, the game of telephone happens in modern companies. From a spoken word to an email to a text message to a passing conversation over coffee to the writing of a draft of a new policy, the idea that started the chain is literally lost in translation.

This is why companies, and their CEOs need unfiltered listening. They need to hear what their prospects, customers, competitors, vendors, shareholders and employees are saying first hand. They need the original message without interpretation or modification.

CEOs must see, read and hear the pain of their customers. They must have the opportunity to engage in conversation or ask more detailed questions of the customers and those who are in contact with the customers so they can get unfiltered answers. There has to be a story of "why" that accompanies the KPIs, charts and graphs. The "why" gives color, tone, and texture to the "what."

In an initial conversation with one of Betsy's Customer Advisory Board (CAB) clients, the CEO began the conversation by telling Betsy that while she trusts her people, she had a feeling in her gut that she needed to hear directly from their customers, unfiltered.

As the engagement progressed, Betsy was informed that the leader of the sales team had been relieved of his duties. In a subsequent meeting focused on recruiting the board members to this new CAB, the CEO expressed dismay that what she had been hearing from the sales leader for some time with regard to several accounts was wildly different than what she heard when she reached out directly to the customers upon his departure.

As we mentioned above, sometimes the priests (those who don't want disruption) will filter information before sharing it with the king for various reasons, including fear of the king's reaction or in an attempt to further their own personal agendas.

As noted in the PERMA section, as a CEO, it's critical to listen in an unfiltered way, not just to the positive emotions, but more importantly, to the negative emotions expressed by customers who have not had the experience that you would want them to have.

To conclude this story, heavy emphasis was put on recruiting the executives of these "in danger" accounts to the Customer Advisory Board in an effort to 1) allow them the opportunity to share their experiences and to be heard; 2) to learn as much as possible from what went wrong and how to ensure that changes would be enacted to prevent these issues in the future; and 3) to identify opportunities to regain the goodwill that was inevitably lost as a result of the filtered messages between the customer and the company.

How Unfiltered Listening Transforms CEOs

Volumes have been written about the power of storytelling for brands. It is a valuable marketing tool that changes minds and transforms industries. It helps companies create indelible memories in the minds of customers and persuades them to be loyal year after year, or in the case of some—like the perennial customer experience favorite, USAA—loyalty can pass down for generations. We even touched on the power of customer experience stories above. If you're not using storytelling in your marketing, you must start now.

But don't stop with your external marketing. Your team needs to use storytelling to market their ideas internally. CEOs need to use stories to tug at the emotions of their teams to get them to act, and they need to encourage their teams to use stories to motivate the C-Suite (and CEO) to act. In the future, companies that use storytelling internally as part of their process to communicate and share information will find they have a distinct advantage over their competitors who stick to slide presentations, charts and graphs.

As much as storytelling helps us make sense of the chaos in our lives, story listening helps us connect with others to understand what really matters to them. Good stories trigger a cocktail of neurochemicals that transform how we see the world and how we act in the world. Dr. Paul Zak's research shows that a well-designed story will cause predictable results in how people will invest their money to help other people.

When we detect something distressful or threatening in our environment, cortisol is released in our body and brain. This causes us to pay attention to and become aware of that which might be dangerous. It moves what was detected by the subconscious to the conscious mind where it can be analyzed in more detail.

As the story unfolds, we feel a surge of dopamine that both rewards us for paying attention and makes us want to keep paying attention. It's addictive and hard to resist. We feel the physiological arousal as we encounter the events in the story with a cause and effect sequence. It makes sense and we want to discover the answers to more of the questions we have.

Finally, there is a rush of oxytocin. We bond with the characters in the story and identify the heroes and villains. We feel empathy and engage in pro-social behavior by taking actions to support certain characters. In fact, Zak found that people who reported feeling empathy in one study, had 47 percent more oxytocin in their blood than those who did not feel empathy. Later studies showed that the elevated levels of oxytocin were predictive of a subject's generosity toward a related charitable cause.

We've found that when CEOs are exposed to the unfiltered stories of their customers, they are suddenly more willing to consider, and often, actually invest in finding solutions to the challenges the customers addressed in their stories. In his paper, *Why Inspiring Stories Make Us React: The Neuroscience of Narrative*, Zak says, *"Narratives that cause us to pay attention and also involve us emotionally are the stories that move us to action."* This is reminiscent of the VAD model and how we are motivated to act when the emotional dimensions align.

Listening to stories changes the chemistry of our brains. It also changes the way our brains operate and as a result, what we focus on and the actions we take.

When a CEO listens to a presentation and reads the slides on the screen in front of him, the parts of the brain related to language processing, like Broca's area and Wernicke's area, engage. But, when the same information is told as a story, many other areas of the brain engage. Brain scans indicate that when words related to a particular sense like smelling pine trees or behaviors like "throw the ball" are read, the regions of the brain that involve those activities also engage. Likewise, emotional words cause one to embody the emotions of the character in the story. In other words, the brain cannot distinguish between the story and reality. The CEO listening to a story, becomes one with the characters in the story. Their experiences and emotions become his own. This creates a desire in the CEO to resolve the challenges faced by the customer.

Good stories bring to life the reality of a customer's experience and it causes the CEO to become, for a moment, the customer having the experience. This bonding with the customer is caused by the neurochemical cocktail that is nearly impossible to resist and the outcome of which is highly predictable. CEOs that want to transform their companies must use unfiltered stories and encourage their teams to use unfiltered.

LEVELS OF LISTENING

We hear through our paradigms. Test this within your own company by asking a cross-section of employees and leaders to read the same customer story and then tell you what the customer's challenges were. Their answers will depend in part on:

- their role in the organization
- the KPIs that matter to their success
- their time horizon of reference, and
- their level of authority to resolve an issue.

Those who deal with transactions, like a retail clerk or customer service agent, will focus on the present and the specific customer in the story. The C-suite will focus on what it means for their department's operations. The CEO is focused on what this means for the customer base now and into the future.

Having an awareness of this will help you see three different levels at which your team is listening and trying to address challenges. These levels are tactical, operational and strategic. We've been warned repeatedly about how siloed analysis and action between departments can lead to poor customer experiences, higher operational costs and failure to execute coordinated efforts. But, most organizations have blind spots that keep them from seeing how their tactics, operations and strategies are not synchronized, or worse, how they are sabotaging each other.

Tactical listening is typically a bottom-up (starting with the front-line employee) approach where the customer makes an inquiry or provides feedback to the company through a email, chat or voice conversation, survey, online review, or social media comment. Companies may monitor and respond to these communications, but most companies limit the number of "official" channels they will respond to and through. Regulatory and privacy issues are often a driver of such decisions, but not always. It is typically at this tactical level that we find voice of the customer programs (VoC) implemented with the goal of capturing, categorizing, reporting and analyzing customer ratings and comments. Most of the challenges detected in tactical listening are issues created by the features of the product or service, or the failure to deliver on a promised benefit.

These VoC programs vary dramatically in their success primarily because they are implemented as a tactical response tool. Goals include: 1) tracking how many times a particular issue was raised by customers and the average sentiment score of these mentions; 2) reducing the number of times the issue is mentioned; and, 3) improving the average sentiment score of these mentions. These tactical goals often create employee behavior that is irrational to the operational and strategic thinkers in the company, and they can be self-sabotaging. One particular case that comes to mind is that of a Fortune 500 company that removed its customer service telephone number from the website and declared a success when the volume of phone complaints decreased. This type of short sightedness is far too common.

Unfortunately, most VoC programs lack the resources (software, analysts and CEO commitment to name a few) to be anything more than what they are. Some visionaries have taken their VoC programs to admirable levels, and they are a beacon to those hoping to create a program that can have a meaningful impact, but these are few and far between. Too many companies have simply re-labeled their customer service teams as "customer experience" teams and they feel like they are successful. It's disappointing that they don't have the awareness to even understand the real difference between customer service and customer experience.

One bright spot we do see is the emergence and growth of customer success teams and programs. These teams are often found in companies with a subscription-based revenue model because they realize that their customer's success has an

Tony Bodoh and Betsy Westhafer

immediate and direct impact on their top and bottom lines. Software-as-a-Service (SaaS) companies have led the way in this arena. The reason we see this as promising stems from their approach to pushing out the horizon. They don't wait for the customer to have a problem and then react. They are using a variety of data sources to detect when customers may be on the path toward a problem or simply not taking the best path to achieve success. Then, they proactively step in to provide some education or advice.

We still consider many of these efforts to be tactical in nature because they are focused on helping a specific customer with a particular challenge at a moment in time. In the cases where these companies step back and analyze their data from a higher order perspective and they make decisions to take actions to alter the product roadmap or impact how they provide service as an organization (both operational), and change their positioning in the market or redefine of the ideal experience their customers will have (both strategic), we see that customer success could be an evolution that moves companies upward and in the right direction.

Operational listening is focused on understanding the challenges customers have a while doing business with the company. While there are a number of causes, some of the most common include siloed data, information and communications. Think of the challenges you have when moving from one channel to another while working with a vendor. The sales team promising more than can be delivered or failing to share their specific promises with the fulfillment team are also common issues. For large companies, like many of our clients, we find that the silos between product lines or divisions can cause significant operational challenges.

Your customers are typically not experts in your business, nor should you expect them to be. This is one of the big problems with an operationally oriented VoC program. You may have teams looking only at one product or feature and never step back to consider the whole relationship the client has with you or how your products and service teams interact in ways that cause challenges for the customer.

Many times surveys are designed to provide tactical feedback by addressing specific transactional moments or touch points. They fail to ask a broad enough open-ended question that elicits the stories that help analysts see the operational opportunities. Also, when relying on technology solutions like text mining platforms, many companies focus on tactical mining or getting alerts related to known words and phrases. These tools are not designed (yet) for analysis across multiple pieces of feedback over an extended period of time.

Some of our most impactful bottom-up analysis for clients comes from the analysis of multiple communications and behaviors that take place over weeks or months. This longitudinal research allows us to see how issues unfold with cause and effect or correlations we cannot see in a single transaction. We have been able to detect specific language that predicts buyer behavior or churn. Until the text and speech mining tools are able to analyze across communication channels, link conversations over time, integrate behaviors with feedback and bring the subconscious patterns hidden in language to light, companies will be limited to tactical research or they will have to invest in well-trained human analysts.

Strategic listening is focused on understanding the challenges customers have within their life, profession or business that the company may or may not be attempting to resolve. The perennial example of this is the product development research conducted for Proctor and Gamble's Swiffer product. Swiffer is essentially a disposal wet wipe on a stick for cleaning floors. They could have commissioned a thousand different tactical or operational listening studies and they would never have discovered the new product opportunity. The team had to go beyond what customers were complaining about related to their existing products, features and benefits (tactical). They had to look beyond the expertise they had as a company in existing product lines like floor detergents (operational). The team needed to step back to understand how they could reposition the company to solve a problem that their customer did not even realize they had—cleaning their house was dirty work. They did this by watching how women cleaned their homes. There are several accounts of the Swiffer story available online if you are not familiar with it. One that we like is, *A Chain of Innovation: The Creation of Swiffer* by Harry West.

It is rare, but not impossible to find strategic opportunities in bottom-up research. We've had the good fortune to do so for several clients. The rarity is due to the limited awareness the front line has of strategic matters, KPIs focused on tactical success and a time horizon that is laser-focused on the present. It is far more common to find strategic opportunities using top-down (CEO directly involved) research using methods that engage the C-suite of your B2B or B2B2C customers. As an example, Customer Advisory Boards, customer dinners, or customer site visits where the CEO has first hand engagement with the customer. But, B2C companies can also engage in top-down research. Take the example of Pepsi CEO, Indra Nooyi, who walked through a store and picked up a case of water, realizing that a mother with children in tow would have a hard time loading that case in her car if she was alone. This impacts product design and packaging, an area in which a CEO needs awareness. She has also observed how women snack differently than men and is adjusting their product offerings accordingly.

Every CEO needs to be aware of the levels of research their company is involved in. They need to take responsibility for championing research at all levels and for initiating both bottom-up and top-down research. Missing out on these will create a scenario in which competitors can pose significant threats.

One CEO's Approach

Shreesha Ramdas is no stranger to life in the C-Suite, and has a track record of success that is envied in his Silicon Valley surroundings and beyond.

As the co-founder of LeadFormix, a marketing automation platform, Shreesha raised the initial funding, built the company and contributed to the successful acquisition by Callidus in January 2012, which was then followed by an acquisition in April 2018 by SAP. Prior to LeadFormix, Shreesha was a co-founder of OuterJoin, an online marketing services company and an early member at Yodlee, where he held the role of General Manager of Yodlee's center.

Today, Shreesha is the CEO of Strikedeck, a growing San Francisco-based startup that offers an integrated customer success platform.

In a conversation with Betsy, Shreesha shared some great insights around the impact that unfiltered and strategic listening by the CEO has on the success or failure of an organization.

"It's absolutely critical to have a buy-in from your customer on which direction you are going. Based on the feedback you are getting, you may realize that the direction you are going may not be the right one, and it gives you an opportunity to course correct. The other reason why this is so important is because the environment is changing so fast. You may have thought about a direction that would have worked six months ago, and in six months, something major may have happened (a new compliance requirement or some other world event that has changed things). So getting regular, frequent, and direct feedback from customers and understanding how those trends are impacting your business will help you navigate any changes that are needed.

"It's very important to involve your customers at this strategic level, and that's the reason that customer advisory boards are critical. When you take your customers for a day or two to an off-site, and they are away from the day-to-day, you have them captive for that amount of time. You brainstorm and hit the whiteboard. You are then getting feedback that is very very important. It's imperative to engage customers in that way.

"I am on the road every single day meeting with customers, understanding what's working, what's not, asking what other things they are seeing in the market. About 65% of my time is spent with customers. This was not the case with my previous startups. I used to spend too much time in the office. This was a big learning for me."

"The more time you can spend with your customers, and the more occasions you have to work for them, the better it will be for the success of your organization."

Shreesha Ramdas
Serial entrepreneur, CEO of Strikedeck

WHAT ARE YOU LISTENING FOR?

Listening is one of the most important skills you need to develop within your team. Not everyone can or will be a prophet. However, you need access to the combined skills of a prophet so your company can thrive long-term. ProphetAbility includes knowing what to listen for in the words and behaviors of your customers.

As shared in the section on PERMA, most VoC programs focus on valence of the emotion. Simply put, negative comments are considered to be bad, positive comments are thought to be good. While you now know there is much more to human emotion than just that single dimension, let's look at the valence of the emotion to consider what you can learn by listening.

Most VoC programs invest their resources in identifying, analyzing, and tracking negative feedback. The belief leaders have is that by fixing what's broken, they will achieve high scores and customer loyalty. Of course, you know that is not accurate. Focusing on the negative alone will never allow you to foresee the future. Prophets don't just look at what's wrong in the present day. They need to look years into the future to share what will happen. This requires more.

Knowing the negative gives you the opportunity to understand why customers are making decisions to break ties with your company. It can give you insights into the promises that were broken and the expectations not met. These comments can help you see where your competitors have outpaced your innovations. They can show you where you've slipped relative to your customer's past experiences. Negative comments can show you where you need to catch up. But, it is rare that they will give you an insight about how to lead. That requires something more.

Positive feedback provides a different perspective. It shows you where you excel and how you exceed customer expectations. These comments describe what customers admire, love and want more of. They help you understand what you can do right now to improve your scores, loyalty and advocacy. And, they give you insights into what customers will consider their baseline for expectations in the future. Companies invest far too little in their VoC programs to understand what they are already doing right.

When you bring together a deep understanding of what your company does well and poorly, whether this feedback is from a bottom-up or top-down research approach (and you'll need both), you will be ready to generate insights that will give you ProphetAbility.

Focus on the negative and you'll get more of that. Emotions are viral and they limit what you are aware of. In a negative emotional state you will see negative possibilities. Recognize that these comments are a thing of the past. They show what your company was days or weeks ago. If you treat them as present, they become present. Don't deny them. Just recognize that they are an expression of desire from your customer for something more than they received. This is why they are valuable. You don't have to focus on fixing things. You can't fix the past. You may have to compensate someone for a poor experience or attempt to make amends, but this is not the real value in negative comments. These negative comments show you what your customers desired. You now know what they were seeking. You know how you can align yourself, your team and your company with their desires.

Positive feedback is evidence that your customers' desires and your products or services were aligned for a moment. You now know what their desires were at the time of the transaction and that you know you can be aligned with it once again. You know that it is possible to be aligned so it is now your job to inspire that alignment between your customers' desires and your product or service again and again.

CONTEXT FOR LISTENING

Your ProphetAbility will be enhanced when you understand the context from which you are listening. Whether you have a tactical, operational or strategic intent and are listening from bottom-up or top-down, the context will aid or prevent your insight generation. Here's an example:

One of the common questions VoC analysts face from executives is, *"Are our customers talking about this?"* Most analysts are too shy, afraid or inexperienced to engage in a discussion or debate with the executive to uncover the meaning and purpose of this question. They have no idea what the context of the question is, so they try make assumptions and attempt to answer questions the executive might be meaning to ask.

When this question arises and we are training analysts, we tell them, *"Examine that question carefully. It is answered with either a 'Yes' or a 'No' and nothing more."* They often protest and claim that's not what the executive wanted to know. We spar a bit to help them realize that they really don't know what the executive wants to know because they do not know the context of the question.

Integrating Quantitative and Qualitative Research

Tony started working in customer research back in 2000 and was thrown into the fire. The company he started working for, a direct marketing company in the financial services sector, had completed a merger with another company and only a handful of the 300 employees remained from the other company. Before completing the merger, the company built a business intelligence (BI) data warehouse with a three-tiered analysis and reporting system. When Tony arrived for work on his first day, his manager shared that they just learned that the system was not actually operational. In fact, the few reports that could be run took about twelve hours and tied up the user's computer the entire time.

From that point forward, Tony was responsible to be the liaison between IT and the business. He had to do the analysis, understand what was needed, translate that to IT, make sure they did their work correctly in designing the data warehouse and then test the reporting capabilities. Tony was in no way prepared or trained for this. So, he picked up Ralph Kimball's book, *The Data Warehouse Toolkit*, and studied it. One of the most impactful tools he found in those pages was the Enterprise Data Warehouse Bus Matrix.

The Bus Matrix is essentially a spreadsheet that provides an organized visual representation of the business areas, processes, measures and metrics on the left side. Across the top are the data dimensions and attributes. In the grid are check marks to indicate what data is being captured at each intersection. The tool is simple and useful.

In 2007 when Tony was implementing his first text mining platform in the hospitality industry, he adapted the Bus Matrix to build a logical structure for the comments customers made on their surveys. He was able to add a third dimension (creating a cube) that added a qualitative factor to the structured data being captured in the existing data warehouse. This new approach enabled the integration of qualitative and quantitative data for VoC programs and has been at the heart of Tony's bottom-up analysis and the way he drives ROI for his clients.

With the integrated quantitative (BI) and qualitative (VoC) data, an analyst can ask hundreds of relevant context-based questions. However, most clients were interested in immediate results and did not plan for the integration of their BI and VoC systems. Even today, most companies do not have integrated quantitative and qualitative data. Their analysts typically focus on one or the other. Seeing the challenge, and the lack of resources, Tony created a simplified solution, The CX Research Matrix™.

The CX Research Matrix

Awareness of the context of a research question (whether bottom-up or top-down) determines the value of the answer. If the CEO asks, *"What percent of our customers complained about fulfillment last month?"* he would receive one answer. But, if he asked, *"What percent of our top ten percent most profitable customers complained about fulfillment last month?"* he would likely get a different answer. The answer to the first may trigger a decision and action planning to improve fulfillment across the board. However, the answer to the second question may trigger the decision to create a white-glove service for the most profitable customers.

In an effort to get the VoC analysis teams up to speed fast and to help them immediately start to integrate quantitative and qualitative data in their research to hone the context of their analysis, Tony created The CX Research Matrix. Down the left-most column of the matrix are the KPIs for the company like profitability, revenue, churn, and productivity. Across the top are five critical areas of the business that impact the customer: Marketing and Sales, Channel, Product, Operations, and Personnel.

This is a universal matrix so these five areas cover most elements of the company but they may be applied slightly differently at each company. You can debate and define where the line is between marketing and channels in one company or channel and operations in another company. The point here is to give you a framework to communicate with and to build success fast.

In the grid you can then fill in multiple questions per intersection. It might help to think of this as a cube. As an example, where profitability and marketing intersect, you could ask your analysts to research <u>marketing and sales themes</u> mentioned by the:

- Ten percent of our most profitable customers last month
- Ten percent of our least profitable customers last month

- Ten percent of our most profitable millennial customers last quarter
- Ten percent of our least profitable millennial customers last quarter

Here's another set of questions you might ask where profitability and personnel intersect. What <u>themes are mentioned about our team</u> by the:

- Ten percent of our most profitable customers last month
- Ten percent of our least profitable customers last month
- Ten percent of our most profitable Gen X customers last quarter
- Ten percent of our least profitable Gen X customers last quarter

It becomes a rather simple exercise. Just consider the part of the business, the metric that matters and the timeframes that matter for you. In a few minutes you can come up with dozens of questions that, when answered, will give you the opportunity to disrupt your competition.

Take a few minutes and try this exercise right now. If you would like, you can download a template at www.ProphetAbilityBook.com.

1. On a sheet of paper or in a spreadsheet list several of the metrics that matter most in your business down the left column.
2. Then across the top of the next five columns list: Marketing, Channel, Product, Operations, and Personnel.

3.   Now, in the grid list some segmentations of customers (top ten percent, bottom ten percent, all customers, generational cohort, sex, geography, frequent buyers, etc.) who you want to know more about their comments.

What did you discover that you're interested in? Which of these questions are most important to get answered? Which could reshape your company or disrupt your industry?

In today's world, where we are ever-connected, it was no surprise when, in conversation about The CX Research Matrix, we discovered that Betsy has a similar approach in her top-down research. She identifies particular customer segments and metrics that matter to the business. She then recruits candidate customers from those segments for the research she and her team conduct. This allows her to expose the CEO and C-suite leaders to customers that match specific criteria so they can generate insights about how to innovate to serve specific segments of their customer base better. Criteria used for this purpose include but are not limited to: industry, geographic location, products/services purchased, annual revenue, competitor information, gender, status of account, and other industry-specific information. The CEOs Betsy works with then hear stories directly from the customers' mouths. They can dig deeper and get to the meaning of the stories. They can learn intimately what matters most to each customer segment, and they can compare differences across customer segments.

HEARING THE CRIES OF THE PEOPLE
PepsiCo: The Visionary Story of Indra Nooyi

When business folk talk about listening to the market, they generally refer to listening for the needs and desires of the consumers of products and services within a particular industry. For Indra Nooyi, listening to the market means much more. It means listening to the needs not only of the consumers, but of the employees, the employees' families and the needs of the world at large. For the PepsiCo CEO, the world is their market.

Nooyi, the company's top leader since 2006, is a straight-shooting, award-winning and ProphetAble leader of more than 260,000 employees worldwide. Since she began her reign at Pepsi in 2001 as the Chief Financial Officer, net profit for the company has risen from $2.7 billion to $6.5 billion. *(Wikipedia)* In *Fortune* magazine's list of most powerful women, Nooyi ranked #1 in 2009 and 2010, as well as earning similar honors by the likes of *The Wall Street Journal*, *Time* and *Forbes*.

Competing in an industry most often labeled as "junk food," Nooyi is out to change that while at the same time, focusing on returning significant value to the shareholders.

"Do you remember campaigns like 'Keep America beautiful'? What about 'Buckle up'? I believe we need an approach like this to attack obesity. Let's be a good industry that does 100 percent of what it possibly can - not grudgingly, but willingly."

Recognized as a leader who strives to not just do business, but do business in a way that is a force for good, this "Hero of Conscious Capitalism" engineered the "Performance with Purpose" philosophy that drives the culture at PepsiCo. As part of this initiative, PepsiCo is focused on making healthier and more nutritious products, protecting the planet by aggressively reducing their environmental footprint, and empowering their employees, all while staying focused on sustained growth for the company.

"When I became CEO in 2006, one of the fundamental beliefs I brought to the role was that corporations don't exist in a vacuum—we are a part of every community where we do business. And I wanted to make sure that

PepsiCo was not only delivering top-tier financial returns, but doing so in a way that was responsive to the needs of the world around us," Nooyi explained.

A classic example of a leader who keeps her eye on the future by listening to those who will create it, Nooyi has implemented programs that focus on the desires of women, millennials, environmentalists, health-conscious consumers, and other larger subsets of humanity not necessarily associated with the snacking industry.

Women

Nooyi stated in an interview with *Fortune* that designing products just for women, a category she believes is ripe for disruption, *"requires reframing the snack category."* Although criticized for early comments she made regarding the differences between the way men and women snack, Nooyi is committed to serving the specific needs of women with regard to their snacking preferences, and employing women to help innovate those products.

"Most companies target women as end users, but few are effectively utilizing female employees when it comes to innovating for female consumers. When women are empowered in the design and innovation process, the likelihood of success in the marketplace improves by 144 percent!"

Millennials

With millennials being known for their deep-seated desires to make the world a better place, Nooyi acknowledges that the entrance of this demographic has forced corporate leaders to *"weave purpose into the core business models"* of their companies. She has since incorporated their philosophies into the fabric of PepsiCo, embracing social issues not only as a good thing to do, but also to help the company attract and retain employees as the workforce changes.

"They no longer look at it as [just] a paycheck. They look at it as 'How can I go to work and make a difference in society?'"

Environmentalists

Growing up in a water-distressed city in India, Nooyi says that the company commitment to protecting the planet is personal, noting that as a child, her family only had about an hour's worth of water in the morning that had to last in order for them to live.

"One of the pillars of our environmental sustainability is reducing the water use in our plants and figuring out how to make the whole community water-positive, bringing our technologies in there, passing on technologies to farmers so they can farm and water their crops in a way that is efficient [to help] conserve water."

Health Conscious Consumers

Executives of food brands are coming to terms with the fact that healthy, clean eating is not a fad, but rather a lifestyle change that is here to stay. PepsiCo heard the call from customers for products that are better for them, and Nooyi has led the shift in the portfolio to include these healthier products. Tropicana Essentials Probiotics, reduced-sugar sodas, and the premium water brand, LIFEWTR are all poised to help PepsiCo address these specific desires of the marketplace.

"More than 50 percent of the beverages we sell in the market are zero or low sugar products. I don't believe there is any other company out there doing that."

Nooyi is a prophet. She hears the call of the gods and she answers that call. She incorporates those messages into her kingdom, and is never satisfied with the anything other than what is best for her people.

CHAPTER 5
DISCERN THE DISRUPTIONS

THE ProphetAbility OF AN INDUSTRY
The Transformational Story of the World of Music

Kid: *"Dad, those are the biggest, blackest CDs I have ever seen."*
Dad: *"Sweetheart, those are called albums."*

This was a real life conversation roughly 20 years ago that a friend of Betsy's had with his young daughter when he was pulling his dusty albums out of the attic as they prepared to relocate to a new home.

Nowhere else can you find such tangible examples of the evolution of an industry as you can in the world of music. Just to name a few innovations:

1877 - Phonograph Cylinder
1889 - Gramophone Record
1898 - Wire Recording
1925 - Electrical Cut Record
1930 - Transcription Disk
1934 - Acetate
1935 - Reel-to-Real Tape
1948 - Vinyl LP
1963 - Compact Cassette
1964 - 8-Track Tape
1969 - Microcassette
1978 - LaserDisc
1982 - Compact Disc (CD)
1992 - Digital Compact Cassette
1996 - DVD-Audio
2000 - USB
2001 - iPod
2003 – BluRay

Near the turn of the century, less tangible forms of music platforms began to emerge, starting with what some industry insiders referred to as the nefarious activities of Napster in 1999.

Napster was peer-to-peer (P2P) file sharing service that made it easy for Internet users to share digital audio files like songs in MP3 format.

While some, mostly artists and distribution houses, feared for the future of the industry with the emergence of "free music," what Napster did was force them to reinvent the manner in which they make money. Quoting from a 2001 ABC news story on the federal court ruling that shut down Napster, Gartner Group analyst Rob Batchelder says, *"There are going to be these thousands of parallel distribution universes. "The genie's out of the bottle. The music business has to re-architect itself."*

He goes on to prophesy:

"Imagine a world where music companies don't make their money from CDs. Instead, the big pop stars make money from concerts, T-shirts, merchandising deals and advertising."

~Rob Batchelder
Gartner Group Analyst

However, Batchelder missed the mark when Johnny Deep, president and CEO of Napster competitor, Aimster, suggested that if the source was good, the content was trusted, and music was very easy to find, Napster users would pay money to access it.

Batchelder disagreed, saying people won't pay a specific monthly fee just for the privilege of downloading music they can get for free. Any security features devised by the music industry will be broken by hackers, he said, and the music will be out there on the Net unfettered.

His assertions can clearly be refuted, as we now have Pandora, Spotify and other popular music services that offer both paid and free subscriptions that allow subscribers to listen to just about any song title a person could possibly want, and with a sound quality that makes for an outstanding and customizable listening experience. According to Statista, there were 106 million paid streaming music subscribers in 2016, a figure that is projected to rise to 336 million by 2025.

If you can't beat 'em, join 'em

In 2014, Taylor Swift, one of Spotify's most popular artists, pulled her music from the streaming service. She had previously refused to release her 2012 album, *Red*, on Spotify after complaining that artists receive a tiny royalty per song play, stating that *"valuable things should be paid for. It is my opinion that music should not be free,"* Swift said at the time.

However, three years later, Swift ended her boycott and put her entire catalogue back on Spotify, as well as rival services Google Play and Amazon Music.

Some artists, on the other hand, actually prefer not making money off the music itself but rather through alternative sources. Take the approach of Chance the Rapper:

"I never wanted to sell my music," says Chance, *"because I thought putting a price on it put a limit on it and inhibited me from making a connection."*

Chance (whose real name is Chancellor Johnathan Bennett) was nominated for seven Grammys in 2017 for *Coloring Book*—

the first ever to chart on the Billboard 200 just from streaming, receiving 57.3 million downloads in its first week alone. He ultimately won three Grammys for Best New Artist, Best Rap Album and Best Rap Performer.

Initially, Chance, who made his first mixtape while on high school suspension for smoking weed in an alley, had a plan to give his music away for free, sign with a label and figure it out from there. But after meeting with three major record labels, he realized that he could make money but still offer his work to his fans for free and with no limits.

"My first two projects are on places where you can get music for free. With Coloring Book, Apple had it on their streaming service exclusively for two weeks for free—and then it was available on all the places my earlier work is still available on," Chance said. *I make money from touring and selling merchandise, and I honestly believe if you put effort into something and you execute properly, you don't necessarily have to go through the traditional ways."*

Some famed gurus tout that traditional businesses should never give anything away for free, as it appears to hold no value if there is not a monetary exchange. However, many companies balk at that notion, offering free downloads, webinars, white papers, and the like. As can be seen through the examples in the music industry, free does not automatically mean there's no value, but is often an innovative approach to engage prospects and customers, leading to purchases that do create the desired revenue.

Much like the music industry provides value for free, think about the amazing story of Facebook, with over 2.2 billion users worldwide who have never paid one thin dime for the privilege. Rather, they generated $40.6 billion in revenue through other sources including advertising, which accounted for over 73% of total revenue in 2017.

"A frustration I have is that a lot of people increasingly seem to equate an advertising business model with somehow being out of alignment with your customers," says Facebook founder Mark Zuckerberg. *"I think it's the most ridiculous concept."*

Chance the Rapper is just one of many innovators in the music industry. He observed the patterns that most musicians followed and identified a way to disrupt the industry. Giving his music away for free creates an opportunity for the audience to hear his music, download it free and then recommend it so it goes viral. He understood that even a dollar could limit the reach of his music. And, by giving his music away, he won millions of fans, some of whom are delighted to pay to attend his concerts and buy merchandise.

Giving music away for free and charging for the concerts is an example of evolving from the Product Economy into the Experience Economy (where companies sell the experience to create a memory) or even the Transformation Economy (where companies sell a series of experiences to help the customer transform). According to a 2017 article by Hugh McIntyre on Forbes.com, *"Chance has earned the bulk of his $33 million from touring incessantly and partnering with brands, and his music is incredibly popular on streaming platforms like Spotify, where at least three of his biggest tunes have been played at least 100 million times."*

With disruption occurring in technology, the economy, and society at an increasing rate, there is an increasing need to develop your company's ProphetAbility so you can detect and discern the disruptions in your industry. To do this, you and your team need to recognize the patterns, determine what they mean, and see the possibilities.

RECOGNIZE AND VALIDATE THE PATTERNS

To create a disruption, you must see and capitalize on an opportunity before competitors do. If you're competing in the Product and Service Economies, that means finding the right combination of features and benefits. Companies competing in the Experience and Transformation Economies need to evoke emotions that create memories and change the customer respectively. Some product-based industries, like the music industry, are evolving so fast that they can no longer rely on products as their core revenue stream.

Two of the reasons we focus on the customer experience so much in this book is because first, the economic value being created through experiences is growing each year, and second, because experiences are ways companies can create disruptions in their industry that are difficult to copy. This latter reason is the case because the environment and conditions that create memorable experiences and personal transformations are in a large part the result of the culture of a company and rely on the employees who work in the company. Once established, culture cannot be easily copied. This will give the companies that seize the opportunity at least a few years' head start. This is why the CEO needs to keep the three to five year vision rolling forward.

The place for companies to start looking for patterns that reveal opportunities for disruption is in the feedback and conversations with customers. Specifically, you should look for what you already do in an excellent manner with consistency. The Admiration Equation can help you identify these opportunities. Consider which three to five experiences are consistently praised by your customer segments as identified in your CX Research Matrix. Customer feedback, reviews, and conversations can be used in bottom-up research. Commentary from customer advisory boards, customer interviews and other top-down research also prove helpful. Once you have a clear vision of what you do that moves your customers to feel admiration, awe and gratitude, then you can see how that compares with your competition.

Depending on your industry, public reviews of your competitors can be a starting point for research regarding their Admiration Equation. You can also research their customers through surveys, interviews and more. One airline company hired a research firm to conduct surveys at the airport and discovered exactly how they and their competitors were perceived. This gave them a baseline to identify where their brand was better than most others and where they needed work. With a little creativity, your company could do similar research.

Besides understanding what is in the customer commentary, you and your team should always be looking beyond what's there. Some of the most powerful insights come from what's not in the feedback. Consider documenting what you expect to see before you start the research. Then, along the way take note of what is missing, because you'll want to explore these ideas later.

It's important to be clear at this point. You should be collecting and integrating quantitative and qualitative data whenever possible. The expectations customers have determine their experiences, and the experiences customers have influence their future purchasing decisions. Therefore, tracking commentary and behavioral measures over time for customers will be valuable. We've used longitudinal studies to determine if existing customers are more likely to terminate their relationship based on their commentary and/or their behaviors. This analysis has been able to show customer comments could predict relationship termination as much as six months before the event takes place.

DETERMINE THE MEANING

Once you isolate a pattern that stands out, you must determine what it means. Not all patterns are valuable, and only a fraction of them can be used to create a disruption. Most research teams never really dive deeply into understanding the meaning because they believe their responsibility stops with the reporting of the findings. They leave it to the product or design teams to determine how to make use of the data. The problem is that the best use of the data requires an understanding of the meaning behind the patterns in the data.

When working directly with customers, one of the most effective tactics for determining the meaning of their comments is asking, "Why?" up to five times. You want to get to the root cause beneath customers' behaviors and experiences. This technique was developed by Sakichi Toyoda for use in the Toyota Motor Corporation. It helped the engineers identify the root cause of the problems they encountered in the production line. Years later it was included in the Lean Manufacturing and Six Sigma methodologies and is now in use around the world. Once you understand the root cause behind a customer segment's actions and experiences, you can design to amplify those experiences which cause admiration, awe and gratitude while minimizing unexpected negative micro-moments.

Another tool that comes out of Toyota is called the Gemba Walk. Gemba is Japanese for "the actual place" and in manufacturing refers to the production floor. Lean Manufacturing experts go on the Gemba Walk through the factory to understand what is really happening and why. We use the Gemba Walk in a similar manner for companies in the Experience and Transformation Economies by walking through that which creates the customer experience. During the Gemba Walk we follow and document: the flow of information, policies, processes, procedures, customer actions through the processes, the employee work and more. This gives us a deep understanding of exactly what the customers and employees are doing to create the experience. The insights we gain often uncover the meaning behind customer comments.

You might be familiar with Customer Journey Mapping and consider it an alternative to the Gemba Walk because it is a popular and helpful tool in customer experience consulting circles. However, too often the practice is carried out in a boardroom on whiteboards, and the team never makes it to where the work happens. They work from head knowledge rather than having the experience of the processes in action. We find greater value in getting hands-on experience with the management team. They tend to buy into the findings because they helped create them during the Gemba Walk.

The Gemba Walk can be leveraged with another methodology used by process improvement experts: The Theory of Constraints (TOC). In simple terms, TOC helps identify the one constraint that is holding back value creation in a company. In a factory, it would be the slowest machine on the production floor. In Experience and Transformation Economies, we have to look to that which impacts the value created in the mind and heart of the customer. The constraint is often the unexpected negative micro-moment experience they have. If you remember the research we shared about the Admiration Equation above, you may recall that these unexpected negative micro-moments also destroy the 5-star experience and prevent admiration, awe and gratitude from being fully expressed. But the constraint could also be the lack of peak emotional micro-moments that create a sticky memory in an Experience business or a similar series of micro-moments in a Transformational business that cause the customer to change how they see themselves and the world in a new, more expansive way. Being aware of constraints during the Gemba

Walk make the time and resources invested in the analysis far more likely to generate an ROI.

Where the Gemba Walk is an internal perspective of the customer experience, there is another type of research that is particularly effective outside of your company, and specifically, in your customer's life or business. This is ethnographic research. P&G used this research when they observed women cleaning around their homes. They studied the habits and practices of individual customers in their own homes. They recorded videos of the women working and analyzed the patterns of their work. They often asked questions to understand why women cleaned the way they did. The insights led to the creation of the Swiffer product line which ranks as one of the most successful household cleaning products ever launched.

You are not likely launching a cleaning product line, but the idea remains valid. Your customer uses your product or service for only a fraction of the day. So, what do they use if for, how and why? What other products or services do they use with it or do they replace it with. What could they do, but don't, with what you offer? What could you do to make their life easier?

When doing this type of research, it is good to put your product or service aside for the moment and consider things from the customer's perspective. Ask yourself, *"What is going on in their life that causes them to do what they do? What could make it better? What is missing that could be there? What can we replace?"*

We are customers 24/7 these days because we are continuously using products, services, having experiences or being transformed. There's plenty of opportunity for you to disrupt the normal habits of your customer's life to improve the quality of their life.

In your search for the meaning behind the patterns, remember to be aware of the five things we all seek as humans: PERMA.

Positive emotions, engagement, relationships, meaning and achievement are often the experiences we are truly seeking whether we can express it or not. You and your team must keep these in mind and observe how you are currently fulfilling these desires and how you could do even more.

SEE THE POSSIBILITIES

Tony had client approach with a serious challenge. They said they were experiencing churn among millennials that was worth $50 million a year. The prevailing wisdom was that these millennials were price shoppers and that there was nothing the company could do to stop them without devaluing their products and services with discounts. The client did not have high expectations but they were willing to see what we could find. They gave us a 30-day window.

We started by gathering the quantitative data from customers who were millennials and split the files between those who were active customers and those who terminated their relationship. Then we matched those customers' records back to any written communications they had with the company for up to a year prior to their termination. We sliced and diced the data. We categorized and mined the comments. We mind-mapped the themes that we discovered.

We did, in fact, find that two of the themes reflected budget issues. One theme related to price shopping, but we found that it was isolated to a specific subset of customers who had recently taken on a new job in a new city and had heard about better monthly pricing from their new social circle. These changes were actually highly predictable because the company knew when they were taking the job and changing their addresses.

The second budget-related theme showed up when a subset of customers did not have the money to use certain features of the product that required a one-time fee beyond the monthly payments. They simply could not afford this new cost at the moment so they decided to terminate their relationship. However, many of these millennials expressed regret or sadness that they had to leave and stressed that it was temporary and not the fault of the company. They just did not have the money to use the product.

The remaining three themes did not directly relate to the budgets of the millennials so the prevailing wisdom was inaccurate in those cases and incomplete in the first two cases.

We decided to go further for our client. We conducted meta-research on a wide range of research papers and reports about the lives, budgets, jobs and habits of millennials. Then, we synthesized the findings of this research with the themes and sub-themes from the customer comments. This allowed us to propose over a dozen new products, services, and experiences that the client could innovate and offer to improve retention of existing customers and the attraction of new customers.

When you have identified the high value patterns in your customer comments and behaviors, and understand what these patterns mean, you can start to look for the opportunities to exploit them. The first opportunity is to create more value for existing customers. You don't need to necessarily give them a new feature or benefit. We recommend looking for possibilities following this prioritization:

1. Enthusiastic customers
2. Engaged prospects
3. Existing customers
4. Exiting customers
5. Elapsed customers

Enthusiastic customers who give top ratings on your internal surveys are potential word-of-mouth marketers. Even better are those customers who provide top ratings (5 of 5) and positive comments on external sources like review sites. You also want to analyze the behaviors and commentary of customers who make referrals that you can track. These customers can help create a viral buzz for your company and influence prospects without you ever knowing it. One of the greatest opportunities with these customers is to ensure that your marketing messages align with their statements of what you deliver in an excellent manner and your operational ability to consistently deliver those experiences in an excellent manner.

Engaged prospects include prospects or customers who are considering a purchase. Many companies find it hard to get data from these individuals because they do not track prospects at the level of detail that customers are tracked. However, the investment in the research in these segments can often reveal slight changes to your marketing message, strategic positioning or tactical processes that dramatically increase your conversion rate. We've worked with clients to research their Enthusiastic customers and then used the findings from that research to update the marketing. We've found that sharing reviews and other social proof increased sales for restaurants, hotels, consulting firms and medical offices. We leveraged that Enthusiastic customer feedback to convert Engaged prospects.

Existing customers who are in the top ten to twenty-five percent by profitability are the next tier to be researched. Understanding what they love and what they find intolerable is essential. It is important to go beyond the superficial reading of comments to really understand why they pay a premium for your products and services. Remember PERMA. These customers hold a key to your strategic positioning that can ensure success long-term. And, if you lose these customers, your company's demise will happen more quickly because your bottom line is exponentially impacted. Don't be surprised if you find some of your most profitable customers providing highly negative feedback even if they give you reasonable customer satisfaction scores. We've seen this pattern with highly loyal customers in the timeshare industry, financial services, consulting companies and even technology providers. The customers are deeply committed to your success because it drives their success, so they want you to know when they perceive you are off-course.

Exiting customers are those who have recently terminated their relationship, like the millennials mentioned above. If you are capturing their communications and tracking their behaviors, these customers can provide the insights that lead to predictive analytics and proactive behaviors that reduce churn. Your focus is not so much to win them back, although you may find ways to do so. The intent in doing this research is to determine which unexpected negative experiences drove them away or which positive experiences they were expecting that you did not deliver at a level that triggered admiration, awe or gratitude. Once you know these themes and the corresponding behaviors, you can determine which segments of customers you would have wanted to keep and which ones you prefer to leave to your competitors. This will give you a way to prioritize your action planning. Never be afraid to lose bad customers. We've seen companies lose money on as much as 35 percent of their customer base year after year and still be unwilling to let them go.

Elapsed customers are the last tier to research. These are customers who have not purchased recently. They may be silent terminations or they no longer need what you provide. You may find a few subsets of these customers who can be re-engaged, but be cautious about investing in attracting these customers back if you don't have solid research that convinces you why they stopped buying and if they are willing to start buying again. In truth, you may never reach this level of research because the previous tiers provide so much valuable information and greater ROI.

You will be able to see the possibilities and act on the opportunities when you consider segments of your customer through their common behaviors like those five described here. Your customer base is not homogenous. Using both bottom-up and top-down research will give you perspectives to consider, and will allow you to evaluate your decisions for day-to-day tactics and long-term strategies for each customer segment and for your company as a whole.

DIVERGENT COLLABORATION^{SM}

As an executive leader, it's one thing to know you have to keep your eyes focused three to five years out, to innovate to stay ahead of the pack, and to ensure that your company can continue to meet and exceed the expectations of your customers. Solving problems that customers have, or may have in the future, has the power to solidify the future for any company.

In order to do that, you must always maintain a culture and mindset of innovation and disruption. A relatively new methodology for leading innovation and solving complex technology challenges is a process that was not developed in the business world but rather in conjunction with the United States Air Force Research Lab (AFRL).

This process, known as Divergent Collaboration (DC), is an innovative approach to problem-solving that uniquely harnesses the power of diversity. It's a capability used to connect individuals from a wide spectrum of domains, backgrounds and areas of expertise into the collaborative innovation process in order to explore a challenge or problem in a new way. It was designed for the Air Force Research Lab but can be utilized by any company or organization that seeks to maximize the power of diversity and collaboration against their most significant business or research challenges.

The idea of Divergent Collaboration grew out of an informal discussion between AFRL's Executive Director, Joe Sciabica, and a local artist at a coffee shop in Dayton, Ohio. They postulated about what might happen if technical people were infused with artistic people in problem-solving activities. They then put this idea into action by conducting a series of DC workshops that were designed and conducted by the Innovate, Demonstrate, Explore, Apply (IDEA) Lab at the Wright Brothers Institute, a non-profit organization charged with helping the United States Air Force and other clients solve their most complex technology problems.

The workshop format was based on WBI's diverge/converge paradigm in which people spend much of their time together diverging on ideas and exploring the problem space in different ways. This is followed by a converge activity in which all of the ideas generated during the diverge process are vetted and culled in an effort to hone in on the most relevant ideas for the specific problem the team is addressing.

According to Dr. Bart Bartholomy and Candace Dalmagne-Rouge, architects of the Divergent Collaboration methodology, as soon as you start thinking of a solution, you unconsciously begin shutting off possibilities for getting a deeper understanding of the problem and therefore of finding a truly breakthrough solution.

In a 2013 article published in the Harvard Business Review, Bartholomy and Dalmagne-Rouge explain that it can often be more productive to avoid "solutions" thinking when a problem arises. It's better, they say, to stay in what they refer to as the "problem space" for as long as possible.

Their advice? *"Force yourself to stay in the problem space as long as possible. Obviously, companies sometimes face real restrictions on the types of solutions they can consider, but often those limits are purely psychological, the result of narrow thinking about the nature of the problem."*

They suggest going really deep to look for the underlying issues, asking, *"What is the essence of that obstacle?"*

Bartholomy and Dalmagne-Rouge further explain:

"Then search for different viewpoints on the obstacle. Go far afield. Look for people who have faced that same essential challenge and tap into their insights. It can be as simple as reading a relevant book or magazine that you've never looked at before. Or call an unfamiliar organization that includes people who face your challenge on a regular basis. Don't be afraid to bring outsiders into the discussion.

"Be thoughtful about the physical environment in which you explore the problem space. A lot of companies do offsites in hotel conference rooms, but those can be mind-numbing. Finding something a little more conducive to exchanging ideas, a comfortable setting where you can get away from your day-to-day activities, form and re-form small groups, write on the walls. And plan the sessions carefully. When it comes to mixing and matching ideas, don't trust to luck. Structure conversations so that they're enriching rather than draining.

"Staying in the problem space, in particular, can be very difficult, but it is worth the effort. If you rush to a solution, you run the risk of solving the wrong problem. The place to get the problem right is in the problem space, where you're more open to new ideas."

More about the workshops

The initial workshops, conducted in 2011, provided such powerful results that the program was trademarked and continues to serve not only the Air Force Research Lab but corporate entities as well.

Each DC workshop lasts two days and the total number of participants for each workshop ranges from 18-22 people. Based on the topic of the workshop, participants are chosen in fields adjacent to the area of interest. One such workshop included a Navy SEAL, an anthropologist and baseball scout. Finding the commonalities among these divergent perspectives is at the heart of the process focused on unlocking solution opportunities.

A robotic surgeon who was a participant in one of the early workshops noted that it's just human nature to get so ingrained in our own world that we don't really look at our own situations other than through the eyes of the people we work with. The Divergent Collaboration process helps change that.

Because there is no ego involved, it allows participants to focus on what it is they do and what they can bring to the table.

The first thing participants are asked to do is question the assumptions that the problem owners have, forcing the problem owners and the group to think about the challenge from different perspectives. As a result, an environment for collaborative problem-solving emerges, resulting in creativity, innovation and novel connections. It helps companies understand that there are new ways of solving challenges that may not have previously been explored and/or considered.

A significant factor in ensuring success in the process is building trust among participants. By incorporating trust-building activities, participants are able to see the interrelatedness within the group.

Building upon the trust-building exercises is the Diverge portion of the program. Various brainstorming exercises are conducted to get the participants to expand and extend their thinking in multiple, lateral, and different directions. These activities are conducted through facilitated brainstorming in small group breakout sessions which are then presented back to the larger group. Participants are exposed to the problem at a high, surface level without the application, context and background of the particular problem or need.

Once participants thoroughly explore the problem space through the diverging exercises, they are then exposed to the actual problem and context. This transition is known as the "lens-shift," and serves to focus the group on the actual problem at hand. Again, through facilitated breakout groups and large group exercises, the participants generate new ideas and also discuss, define and refine ideas into insights that may influence and invigorate new and existing ideas for the company. These ideas and insights, the product output of the workshop, also include directions and opportunities for the company to explore.

Organizations throughout the country utilize this third-party facilitated process to incorporate creativity and diversity into solving critical challenges for themselves and their customers while innovating for the future.

YOU'VE GOT A FRIEND IN ME
Pixar: The Divergent Collaboration Story of Failure, Bounce Back and Success

(Adapted from a video produced by Bloop Animation)

The story of Pixar has just as many twists and turns as do the movies they produce, and just as many interesting characters.

Consider that the eventual success of Pixar was the result of three people, from very divergent backgrounds, coming together to do something that had never been done before.

There was the artist, John Lasseter, the Academy Award winning director of some of Pixar's most successful movies, including "Toy Story."

There was the scientist, Ed Catmull, who earned his doctorate and was a pioneer in the field of computer imagery, credited with inventing 3D graphics as we know it.

And there was the businessman, Steve Jobs, who at the time had just been fired from Apple, the company he had given birth to.

It all started with John Lasseter's dream of producing the first full-length computer animated film. While working in his dream job as an animator for Walt Disney Animation Studios, Lassiter pitched the idea for a full-length animated film to the executives at the studio. He was unexpectedly fired shortly after he made the pitch. Apparently Disney didn't see the vision of using computers for animation rather than the traditional pencil methods.

At the time of Lassiter's firing, Catmull was working at Lucas Films. The pair met at an industry event and discovered that they shared the same dream of someday creating the first feature-length computer animated film. Catmull asked Lassiter to join his division at Lucas Films, and with that decision, their dream, although still a long way off, was finally heading in the right direction.

The Computer Graphics Division in which they worked at Lucas films laid the foundation for their dream by producing some notable, exclusively computer-generated scenes, as well as the first animated short film using computer animation. The name Pixar was chosen as the new name for the division, taken from the name of the high-powered computer used to create their art.

Their employer, George Lucas, much like Disney, had no interest in the vision of a full-length animated feature film, so funding was not available through the studio for this massive undertaking. With that, Steve Jobs, who had moved on to his post-Apple endeavors, had been contacted regarding an investment in Pixar. Rather than just invest, Jobs bought Pixar for $5 million and kicked in an additional $5 million to keep the lights on.

Despite this influx of cash, Pixar continued to struggle financially, looking for others ways to generate revenue including licensing their software and securing commercial clients including Trident and Tropicana. Not only that, they stepped into the world of medical imaging, seismic imaging and even began selling off some of their assets. At this point, Steve Jobs was losing roughly $1 million a year for five consecutive years. Yet throughout their financial challenges, they continued to produce outstanding animated short films, and even won an Academy Award in 1988 for "Tin Toy."

In an interesting turn, Disney took notice of Lassiter's success in creating these films and extended the invitation for him to return to Disney to direct a feature film. As intriguing as the offer was, Lassiter declined in order to pursue his passion with Pixar.

But Lassiter knew that if he was going to realize his dream of a computer-animated feature film, he couldn't go it alone. He would need distribution and marketing help, and the logical choice was none other than Disney. He approached Disney and they agreed to go in on this joint venture.

But Disney, with years of expertise in animated films, weighed in heavily on how it was to be done, which was not in sync with the vision of the team at Pixar. Despite wanting to do things differently than what had previously been done at Disney, the Pixar team worked for over a year to produce a preview of what would eventually become "Toy Story," incorporating the direction they had received from the powers that be at Disney. Unfortunately, it simply didn't work and Disney shut down production the next day.

But not to be denied, John Lasseter reworked the film with his own thumbprint and screened it a second time with Disney. This time it worked and production ramped back up. Five years later it became the highest grossing film of 1995, making $362 million worldwide. Three Oscar nominations later, Lassiter was awarded a Special Achievement Award for making the first computer-animated feature film, his lifelong dream.

But here comes another twist. Pixar made very little money on the film, as the terms of their agreement with Disney were quite unfavorable for the small studio. Not only did they not make money on the film, they had no rights to the profits from the merchandising.

Still struggling financially, Pixar decided to go public, becoming the largest IPO of 1995, raising $132 million. After this, they were able to negotiate with Disney from a much stronger position, and inked a deal to produce five more films together over the next ten years, equally sharing the profits.

The roller coaster ride for Pixar doesn't end there, however. When the contract was up with Disney, the wheels seemed to fall off of the relationship, which was particularly troubling to Lassiter, as Disney had the rights to make sequels to all of the Pixar films made during their collaboration. But as luck would have it, Disney went through a leadership change around the same time, with Bob Iger taking over. During his first week in his role as President, Iger called Jobs to suggest merging the two companies together.

While understandably there was real trepidation by the folks at Pixar, Steve Jobs felt that it was the right thing to do and that the companies could work well together moving forward. Disney bought Pixar for $7.4 billion, making Jobs the largest shareholder at Disney. John Lasseter was named the Chief Creative Officer for both companies and Ed Catmull secured the top spot of Pixar and Disney Animation Studios.

And everyone, including generations of children around the globe, lived happily ever after.

CHAPTER 6
INSPIRE DECISIONS

In his book, *To Sell is Human*, Daniel Pink points out that one out of nine American workers are salespeople. But he doesn't stop there. The premise of the book is that nearly everyone is involved in non-sales selling. According to his research we spend, on average 40 percent of our time at work *"persuading, influencing and convincing others in ways that don't involve making a purchase."* That's 24 minutes of every working hour. When Pink dug deeper he found:

- Nearly 37 percent of respondents devoted a significant amount of time to "teaching, coaching, or instructing others"
- Thirty-nine percent said the same about "serving clients or customers"
- Nearly 70 percent reported that they spend at least some of their time "persuading or convincing others"

We should not underestimate the value of non-sales selling. Pink's research also revealed that this time was considered to be very important to the respondents' professional success. We have both seen this to be true in our careers. Set traditional selling aside and we spend a vast majority of our days in non-sales selling. We are trying to persuade, influence, convince, coach and serve our clients and our teams. Often we do this by constructing a narrative and telling a story that appeals to the audience we are trying to move.

One skill that prophets and CEOs must have in abundance is the ability to influence and persuade. They need to sell people on the ideas they have and on the decisions that must be made. The best way to influence people to buy into an idea and a decision is through storytelling.

We've already examined the role of storytelling as a part of the human experience that helps us make sense out of our conditions and choices. We've also given some time to explain the power of listening to the stories of your customers and how it can transform you and your team. In this section we build on what you've learned and look at the seven steps that can help you create stories that influence transformation in your company from bottom-up (front line to the CEO) or from the top-down (CEO to the front line).

These seven steps are abbreviated and come from a course called *Storytelling with Your Data* that Tony has been teaching since 2013 to executives of Fortune 500 companies, analysts working in award winning VoC programs, consultants, lawyers and even the technology executives at TDWI's world conference. The course takes participants through the seven steps from the perspective of how to do their research and then, reorders the steps so they can tell a compelling story on as little as one slide. In this book, we will keep it simple and walk through the steps from the perspective of the storyteller so you can transform your presentations so they inspire action.

STEP 1: CREATE THE HOOK

We've all been duped into clicking a clickbait link because the title is so enticing. We know it's clickbait, but we still can't stop our hand from tapping the link. Moments after the page loads our rational brain kicks in and we say, *"Why in the world did I click that?"*

Like clickbait, if you are going to get the attention of your audience, you need something true and compelling to attract the subconscious mind and get the emotions firing and body committed to action. Researchers discovered that we make decisions to take action subconsciously before our rational brain can even process what's happening. There are some cases where the decision is made three to seven seconds before the person is aware that they made a decision. In fact, our reason will invest resources to justify the decision that was made rather than ask if it was the right decision.

We navigate throughout our day operating essentially in an automatic mode. Our subconscious mind is monitoring the data streaming in from our senses and body. Then, when something unusual or unexpected appears, it sends an alert through one of many circuits in the brain to determine how the body should react, immediate and automatic or delayed and thoughtfully. This is similar to what happens when we click on an enticing title online.

That same circuitry can be used to capture the attention of your audience. Return to the section above where we discussed the three-dimensional model of emotions, Valence Arousal Dominance. This model has been used to show why some news article titles are more viral than others. Researchers found that the valence of the emotions triggered by viral articles was generally more positive or complex (positive and negative) while also involving both high arousal and high dominance emotions. This cocktail caused people to take action like clicking on or sharing the article. When you want to hook your audience, consider how your title and opening comment can be emotionally charged in the same way. Engage the emotions right from the start.

Here's an example that made it to the CEO of a Fortune 500 client, *Top 5 Reasons for $500 Million in Cancels*. It promised a short list, with explanation for a shockingly large number and implied there might be a resolution to a serious problem. Not all titles may be this bold, but they must capture the attention and engage the audience.

STEP 2: SIMPLIFY YOUR THEMES

CEOs and their C-suite team are smart. But, with the amount of information they are inundated with daily, it can be challenging to process what is right in front of them. Simplify everything you are about to tell them. Keep it to a sixth grade level. This won't insult them; they will actually understand it better. The clarity of language will help them feel more secure and confident when they are asked to make a decision.

One of thing to remember when you are telling a story is that you should walk in your audience's shoes. Think about what the story feels like to them and what questions it may raise. Consider the challenges they face and what they believe. You must challenge their observable and hidden beliefs if you are to hold their attention and convince them that change is necessary. If you don't address these beliefs directly and openly, they may silently veto any decision you want them to take. This is why you must anticipate their objections, concerns and questions.

Remember, this is non-sales selling. We typically recommend providing three or five key points in your story. If you only have a short amount of time and/or limited slide space, keep it to three points. We coach executives through the creation of a single slide to communicate all seven of these steps for three key points. The single slide (or page) makes it simple, like a dashboard, so the eyes can dart around the page and connect all the dots. No page turns. No committing facts or figures to memory. Just look around the page and think about how it all connects to make sense.

> *"If you can tell your story in five words, for God's sake,
> Kids, don't use 10."*
>
> ~Betsy's Journalism School Professor

STEP 3: TELL A GOOD STORY

We've already covered storytelling extensively in the earlier chapters. We encourage you to go back to those sections for a detailed review. Here we will remind you of a few key points.

Be sure to use a story structure like the three acts or Pixar structure. The structure is something that we are wired to expect and engage with. The cause and effect narrative helps us make sense of the elements in the story. Remember to engage the emotions with peaks and valleys so the audience can feel the change, be immersed in the story, and be focused with anticipation while waiting for your next point. Finally, leverage the Admiration Equation. Include multiple, multi-sensory micro-moments throughout the story so that the audience is immersed.

STEP 4: SHOW THE EMOTION

On a Saturday morning in July of 2013, Tony was catching up on customer experience industry news. While reading an article that reported on how CEOs were not championing VoC or CX programs he about lost it. He shared the article with a friend and said, *"This article is a perfect example of why CEOs aren't buying into VoC and CX. There's no emotion, just facts and figures!"*

This problem continues to plague the industry. It could be that customer experience professionals are just trying to fit into their corporate culture that turns up its collective nose at the use of emotions in reports. Or, maybe they simply don't understand that their CEOs and the executives they support *are their customers and need to be emotionally engaged to make decisions.* While we hope it is the former because a dose of courage or maverick spirit could change that, we suspect it is the latter based on the high rates of shock and awe we experience when we speak at conferences or tweet about using emotions to engage and motivate CEOs to make decisions.

When you are telling your story, whether up, down or peer-to-peer, use every tool you can to evoke emotions.

Use actual quotes from customers that make the point. Here are a few quotes from clients when we shared research findings in the form of a story:

> *"It changed when we 'brought' the customer in the room."*
> ~Jodi, Director Decision Science Analytics - Fortune 500 financial services company

> *"Oh, this is why wife does this! Now I understand why."*
> ~Roger, CMO – Fortune 500 insurance company

> *"The story was the proof that the concept was real."*
> ~Vinny, CEO – Startup in the music industry

If you have a picture of a real customer or a picture that amplifies the emotion of the story or quote, use that. For an auto insurance company we worked with, we used a picture of two cars crashing on one report. While working with a bank whose customers with tight budgets were complaining about how the fees were making it hard to pay their bills, we showed a hammer smashing a pink piggy bank.

We've worked with clients who are delivering reports as a live presentation. When possible we have them include audio files from phone calls. If that is not possible, we have the presenter take on the persona of the customer while reading written feedback. This has a particularly powerful effect on the executives in the room.

In one Customer Advisory Board meeting in which Betsy was involved, the host company showed a video they had produced to their executive-level customers that dramatically illustrated their organizational mission to fight human trafficking. The level of emotion that the video produced for both the host company and the customers was extraordinary, and illuminated the passion of the company to make the world a better place. This commitment, captured with emotion and shared with the customers, made a profound and memorable impact.

Repetition, novelty, intense emotion and focus are the four ways our brains create pathways by connecting neurons. The neurochemicals that are released in the moments of the experience are particularly effective at building a sheathing around the new connection. In non-scientific terms this means that we have new insights and remember them long-term. Coupling all four of these methods that cause learning together makes them even more impactful. Repetition happens through the use of multiple modalities. We create novelty through uniqueness of the presentation. Intense emotion is felt through the customer's words and sound of the voice. Focus is established by the evoking anticipation of discovery.

There's one other fact to remember about storytelling. When we read or listen to the emotions of a character in the story, we mirror their emotions internally and we embody how they feel. If you want your team to feel what the customer feels without leaving the boardroom, you have to bring the customer into the room through their words.

STEP 5: PROVE IT WITH DATA

We finally made it to the data step. While you will start your research with the data, when you tell the story, it is only a supporting actor. In fact, if you tell the story well, the executive team will hardly give the data a glance. If you're a data junkie, this may be a hard pill to swallow. We know because we both had to. We ask you to not stop reading if you are offended by the next two paragraphs. Suspend your judgment momentarily and give us a few pages to make our point.

Here's where we differ from most "data storytellers." We actually want you to tell a story with words and pictures and such. Fancy visualizations and charts might be helpful, but they should not be the core of your story. Why? Simple. First, humans are really bad at statistics so they will likely make a mistake interpreting your data when you're not around. Second, charts and graphs are too easy to manipulate to make things appear other than they really are. Third, a chart or graph is not memorable.

On the other hand, humans have been telling and listening to stories for thousands of generations. Most of us have some storytelling skills which can be developed relatively easily. Simple stories with themes can be told and retold with relative ease, and an executive can be challenged if they intentionally or accidentally manipulate storyline without anyone needing a special degree. Finally, we are wired to remember and retell stories.

Back to the data. There are three essential steps to take when you are sharing the data side of your story.

Start by deciding which metric you want to improve. You should do all of your research through the lens of this metric. We do not recommend just researching customer comments or asking broad questions of a random sample of customers on a customer advisory board. You are not just trying to find out what any customer thinks, feels or says. You want to know what a specific segment of customers think, feel or say who impacted a metric because of their behavior. If they are not in your sample population or your control population for research on your chosen metric, they don't matter right now. Maybe this sounds harsh, but it isn't. Here's why:

We are talking about research that moves the strategy, operations and tactics of the company. Our emphasis is not on reactive responses to customer issues. This is the responsibility of the customer service team, not the research team attempting to prophesy what your future could be. This work demands laser-focus and precision measuring. It is scientific. And, it can be expensive, so you must have a well-defined scope if you expect to create real value for customers that then generates a significant ROI for your company. This is why we shared the CX Research Matrix earlier in the book. You can create questions that have a specific target and get exact answers to your questions.

Once you've shared the metric you intend to move, you must have the comments (or stories) for each customer segment parsed, categorized and sorted so they are organized. This allows you to demonstrate the theme with examples if required. It also makes it easy for your team to connect the story elements with the data elements in your presentation. This allows your executives to reconstruct the story when they review it later on their own. They can make the story their own and retell it with confidence. This is essential if you want the story to go viral across the company.

In case you thought we were arguing against any data visualization a few paragraphs back, here's where we will hopefully redeem ourselves. Yes, data is absolutely essential to understand the story, but, as we stated above it cannot be the story. You should have key data elements available on your slides or in your report, but set them back. Let the story do the convincing. It will make your data far more compelling.

Visualizing the data is important. When you visualize your data, be sure to integrate both the quantitative and qualitative data where possible. Quantitative data could include how many customers attempted to go through a process and how many succeeded or failed. The qualitative data for the same process might be what customers said their problem was or how they felt about the process. This makes your story more powerful and makes the data an integral part if the executive teams need it. Here are a few ways we've done this with clients:

1. Show a chart of the cost of churn by the top themes associated with churn
2. Show a customer decision tree of the sales process with each touch point notated with the top three themes of comments from non-buyers versus buyers
3. Show a workflow of a billing process that notes the percent of transactions that were defects and the top complaints by theme at each step of the process

Keep the analysis simple by keeping the focus on the one metric you are attempting to improve with the research. Keep the story simple with integrated quantitative and qualitative data. Make it easy for anyone to tell the story with or without the data. Remember, ProphetAbility is not about just seeing what went wrong in your customer experience and fixing it. It is the ability to see how you can do something that will disrupt your market or industry and give you a competitive advantage now and years into the future.

STEP 6: INSPIRE POSSIBILITY THINKING

Near the end of every report you should include a possibility question. It inspires executives and makes them curious. These emotions get them ready to make a decision because they are in positive state (valence) and focused (arousal). When structured properly as a question, it can also make them feel like you are handing them control (dominance). Together this emotional cocktail primes them to make a decision which is what you need.

Your question should challenge their comfort zone, but not too much. Imagine them going 3-5 percent beyond what they are comfortable doing right now. Too far and they will step into disbelief or maybe even stumble forward into overwhelm. Not enough and they'll be apathetic and uninspired.

When you ask the question, be prepared to provide support to help stabilize their belief systems. Think of the scaffolding that is around an old building as the contractors are renovating it. The old walls are supported with temporary supports until they can be permanently anchored. Your team needs this type of support.

Carol Dweck's research on the mindset of success reveals that if we don't believe we can learn and grow, we will be stuck in a fixed mindset and we won't even try. But, if we believe we can learn and grow; if we believe our goal is learning how to do the thing we set out to do; and, if we believe that the effort involved in learning and growing makes us stronger, we will adopt a growth mindset and take on tougher challenges for a longer period of time.

Scaffolding might be three milestones that you will cross on the way to your goal. It can be shared in a way that evokes emotions and sensory engagement. It should be specific and measurable.

As an example, let's say your company has a 20 percent churn rate. Your inspiring question could be, *"What could we invest in if we reduced churn by 10 percent?"* Then you could build the scaffolding by having milestones like, *"Imagine at a 2 percent reduction, we would be able to invest in one additional marketing campaign during the holiday season which will raise sales by $1 million. When we hit the 5 percent reduction mark, we can hire three more sales people and open a new region in the west. When we hit the 10 percent mark, we will all get our top-level bonuses."*

STEP 7: SHOW THE PATH TO SUCCESS

The previous six steps in the non-sales selling process create the conditions for this last step. While the emotions are flowing and your team is synchronizing into one mind, you must lay out a path to success which includes clear and specific recommendations followed by a call to action. Make no mistake, this is the moment of the close.

Far too many researchers who are employees stop their reports and presentations at the findings. Through conversations with these brilliant individuals, we've learned that they often don't believe it is their place to make recommendations. They believe they should stay clearly on their side of the wall and simply pass over what they learned to the operations teams or to their leaders. This is a mistake.

Most operations people will do one of two things with findings that are not followed by recommendations. They will file the report away and forget about it because they have no idea how to apply it; or, they will make decisions on how to apply it and never validate their assumptions with the research team. We've both seen far too many strategic, operational and tactical changes made without the researchers involved. These efforts are misguided and a waste of precious capital. They can also set the company or a product line back for years.

The researchers need to step out of their comfort zone and provide recommendations for applying their findings. The strategy and operations teams need to invite in and ask for guidance from the research teams as they develop new strategies, products, services and experiences. To do this with our clients, we've borrowed another concept from Toyota called obeya, which means "big room" in Japanese.

In the obeya, members of different teams gather to collaborate and focus on solving specific challenges while being surrounded by visual management tools. Toyota invented the obeya in 1994 when they were developing the Prius. It helped them speed the flow of information and decision-making which resulted in a rapid acceleration of taking an idea to product launch. For Toyota, this meant reducing the industry average 24-month design cycle to as little as ten months.

Lest you jump ahead to create your obeya before you finish presenting your research, let's take a step back for a moment. Your research team must have enough confidence to make initial recommendations. Confidence comes from competence. This means the researchers will have to develop some level of expertise in the processes they are analyzing or they will have to partner with operations team members who are subject matter experts (SMEs) in the specific areas affected by the research. Working together is an effective way of building bridges from bottom-up before the research is presented to the C-suite. The same can be done from top-down if the C-suite members are willing to have conversations and partner rather than have silos which they protect with a moat and turf wars.

FROM AUTOMAKER TO TECHNOLOGY PIONEER
The Bounce Back Story of General Motors

Of all the stories of transformation, the GM story is perhaps the most compelling.

A look back in time tells a bleak story for the behemoth American automaker, which had gone from being known as America's greatest and most influential company to headlining the "most important bankruptcy in US history." When closing out 2008, the 100-year-old company was in the red a staggering $30.9 billion.

Having been plagued by high-profile cases of deaths related to flawed ignition switches, managing one of the deadliest auto recalls in history, an economic meltdown of seismic proportions, the subsequent government bailout, and the impact felt by filing bankruptcy, it's hard to imagine how a company as beaten up as GM could possibly rebound. But rebound it did.

Enter Mary Barra

As the first female CEO of a major automaker, Mary Barra is a status quo breaker who surrounds herself with smart and innovative prophets who maintain an eye for what 21st century customers want. As a result, the company has gone from an old school boys club content to keep doing what had been done for decades, to emerging as the leader in the electric car race, outpacing Tesla to produce an electric vehicle (EV) that can go up to 200 miles on a single charge and costs less than $30,000.

What's intriguing about Barra shaking up the culture at GM is that she has GM blood running through her veins. The daughter of a retired blue-collar GM veteran, Barra started her career at the age of 18 as a co-op student in 1980 and rose to the top when she was named Chief Executive Officer in January of 2014.

For Barra, who shed multiple unprofitable GM operations around the globe and shifted the focus from automaker to technology company, the real impetus for change is deeply rooted in doing what's right for the customer.

"Driving change is not about being an insider or outsider; it's about driving the GM team to be the best we can be. It all starts with focusing on the customer and doing what's right for them."

~Mary Barra
CEO, General Motors

With a deep understanding of the changing desires of customers, who are now super-connected to technology, Barra and her team are out in front and have mind-blowing push goals. With connected cars, autonomous vehicles, ride- and car-sharing, and electrification, GM is pursuing all of these to ensure that they are the industry leader moving forward.

Since being promoted to CEO, Barra has led game-changing initiatives including the long-range, mainstream-priced Chevy Bolt EV, the development of the Maven service (car sharing) and has pumped $600 million into Lyft, a ride-sharing service. Additionally, in its relentless drive for innovation, GM has developed its first near autonomous system, the Super Cruise, which goes head-to-head with Tesla's AutoPilot System. In 2016, GM bought San Francisco-based Cruise Automation for just under $700 million. In June of 2018 SoftBank Group Corp.'s tech-oriented Vision Fund invested $2.25 billion in Cruise Automation confirming the direction GM is headed.

Notably, all of the above are rooted in their unwavering commitment to the customer.

"We have always had a strong research and development team at GM, and that strength has made us an industry leader when it comes to generating ideas, patents, inventions. But that's just the start. Equally important is taking our ideas and inventions, identifying those that make a real difference for our customers, quickly getting them into our products. That's real innovation, and that's our primary focus at today's GM. This allows us to tie R&D more closely to the bottom line and, more importantly, directly to the customer. At the same time, we're continuing to look for long-term solutions and technological breakthroughs in areas like advanced propulsion—research that will drive our customers, and the industry, far into the future."

All of this is not to say that Barra doesn't have a heartfelt respect for the history of the company that has provided not only her livelihood, but also that of her father. She consistently pushes her team to recapture the innovative spirit and leadership that defined the company throughout much of its reign.

"Not everything needs changing. Some things need protecting. And that can be just as important, challenging and rewarding as changing the world."

~Mary Barra
CEO, General Motors

But there's no overstating the transformation that has taken place since Barra took the top spot.

According to Barra:

"Today's GM is dramatically different than it was several years ago. We have fewer, stronger brands; better product quality; higher, more consistent spending on new products and technology; less corporate complexity; consistent profitability; a fortress balance sheet and much more. But by far the biggest change in recent years, the thing that makes us a more responsive and exciting company, is our clear focus on the customer. Throughout GM, we are working to incorporate the voice of the customer into everything we do—before, during and after the sale. Our goal is to offer our customers everything they want, need and deserve every time they buy a GM product or service."

So how does Barra get her unfiltered information about the customer in order to make her strategic, bold and innovative decisions? The old-fashioned way, that's how. She makes visits to dealers. She visits with the customers in the showrooms. She sits in on calls to the call centers. She walks the manufacturing floor. She makes herself accessible.

"Our goals are aggressive, but we have the right team and a commitment to stay focused on safety and quality, and to push ourselves to keep innovating. We must work together —as one GM team—to put our customers at the center of everything we do.

CHAPTER 7
PIVOT TOWARD DISRUPTION

The decision to pivot your company toward disruption obviously requires that you disrupt the norms in your industry and market. To do so means you must disrupt the behaviors within your own company. And to accomplish that, you have to disrupt the beliefs, habits and emotional state that you and your team accept as normal.

This is a bold move and it will transform your company and every person in your company. It will cause some people (employees, vendors, shareholders and customers) to leave. You will attract new people who find the new direction and vision compelling. The transformation required for you to create a disruption will be...disruptive.

QUICK ACTION VS. TRANSFORMATION

The results you are experiencing today are the outcomes of behaviors—habitual, unintentional or intentional—of yesterday, last week or even last year. In our experience, when CEOs are moved by the stories told by their customers, they typically make decisions, start giving directives and take action. They want results quickly. In some cases we've helped them get results quickly.

Focused, quick actions that generate measurable results are valuable for three reasons. The action makes it clear that the direction is changing. The results build a new belief about what is possible and enable buy-in from the team, customers and shareholders. The speed gives you a lead on the competition who will be at least a few steps behind you by the time they realize what's happened. We've helped several executive teams take quick action. We recommend it. But, that cannot be your entire strategy if you want to pivot toward disruption.

Disruption demands more than action. It demands that you change who you believe you, your company and your team are. It demands a transformation not just of processes and products, but the transformation of people. You have to become more than you believe is possible for you, and you have to help each member of your team do the same. Then, to be disruptive, you have to help your customers believe they can be, do and have more than they currently believe is possible for themselves.

You are not disruptive because you say you are. Disruption happens only when you help enough customers believe that they experienced a transformation and reached a new normal, and as a result, tell others about their growth so influentially that the market shifts in your favor. Disruption is visible when customers decide they will never go back to their old behaviors and stop buying from your competitors who are doing things the old way and attempting to satisfy the needs of those customers who have not yet transformed.

Disruption requires transformation and transformation takes time because it involves people willingly challenging and changing what they believe about themselves, how the world works, and their role in the world. It takes commitment to hold an emotional state that is illogical based on the visible results. In essence, people must choose to be positive that change is possible before there is any evidence that the change is really possible. This is why so few companies ever create disruption and why so many people struggle with transformation.

FRICTION BETWEEN DESIRE AND BELIEF

We demonstrated early in this book the five experiences that humans seek for their own sake using the PERMA model created by Dr. Martin Seligman. Humans have a burning desire for positive emotions, engagement or flow, authentic relationship and human connection, a meaningful life, and accomplishment or mastery. Each one of us could write a list of these desires and the many forms they take in our hopes and dreams. To the best of our knowledge humanity has always had desires that are greater than what they have realized. This is worth examining.

Why are humans, throughout all of recorded history, pulled by desires that seem to be part of our nature yet we seem unable to be, do and have what we long for? Our conclusion—guided by science—is that we don't believe we can be, do or have what it is we desire. Don't let this slip by you. It is a fundamental challenge of the human condition. We desire that which we don't believe we can acquire.

This is why we need to transform. First we must transform our beliefs about who we are before we can learn and grow into the people who are being, doing and having that which we desire. This is the problem you have, your team has, and your customers have.

For over 100 years business gurus have taught us to understand the needs, wants and desires of our customers. More recently, customer experience experts told us to satisfy our customers, make it easy for customers to do business with us, to focus on getting them to promote us to the family and friends, and to make them happy. And, that has worked to some extent in the Product, Service and Experience economies. But, it will not work in the Transformation Economy.

Today, companies must focus on helping customers believe they can become the people they want to be, and as a result do the things they want to do, and as a result of that, have the things they want to have. To achieve this, we must first change what we believe about ourselves as leaders, and then help our teams change what they believe about themselves as a team and as individuals. The change in beliefs will allow you to realize your desires. Who you and your team become as you deliver 5-star experiences and disrupt your market are infinitely more valuable than the increased sales and customer loyalty.

YOUR NEXT THREE STEPS

The tension between what we desire and what we believe is possible is strangely necessary, even while we may find it painful or unpleasant. The contrast between what we desire and what we believe throws into sharp relief, our experience of the moment. What we experience in this moment directs or dictates our decisions in this moment. These decisions set us on a course of action that produces our future results. This is true whether we consider it as a CEO, employee or customer. Experiences create our future results.

How can we change what seems inevitable? There are three steps CEOs and their teams can apply:

Step 1: *Focus on clarifying and documenting the contrast between the experiences you, your team and your customers are having versus the ideal experience that is in your mind.*

We've shared much about how to analyze from top-down and bottom-up to identify the current state of your experiences. Here's a simple way to identify your ideal experience. The notes you take during this exercise contain the ideal experience, and you can use this to compare with the real experiences you and your team have discovered. The gaps will be evident.

Imagine you are sitting in a coffee shop. At the table behind you there is a conversation happening between two people who had an amazing experience with your company. Write down the stories you hear them telling and pay particular attention to the details of the emotions and the transformations that happened. What did they believe before and after the experiences?

Most companies stop here and react by trying to resolve each single customer or employee issue tactically, rather than moving to the level that enables true transformation. They never make it to the next step and never succeed in disrupting their markets.

Step 2: *Focus on the sourcing solutions that address the beliefs that are holding you, your team and your customers back from realizing your desires to be, do and have.*

Look back to your notes about the ideal experience you imagined hearing in the coffee shop. What beliefs were revealed in the stories you heard? How did those beliefs change as a result of the experience? What did you or your team do to create the experience that changed these beliefs?

Consider also the stories you heard through the analysis about the current experiences your company is actually evoking. What did people believe they would experience? What did they really experience? When they had amazing experiences, what did they come to believe? What did you or your team do to create the experience that changed these beliefs?

Most of the companies that make it to this step never go any further. Their leaders may take some action and direct some resources to solution identification and testing, but they fail to commit or persist long enough for the transformation in beliefs to take hold within the company and within the customer base. The executives declare the effort a failure and revert to reactionary behaviors and old beliefs. The declaration of failure becomes a self-fulfilling prophecy, that their beliefs that they could not be, do or have more were in fact correct. They give up.

Step 3: Focus on releasing resistance to the new beliefs that you are holding.

This is an emotional battle for many CEOs and their teams. The old limited beliefs are so embedded and the old feelings of struggle are so familiar and even addictive that they cannot maintain a positive state of emotions regarding new possibilities so they abandon it.

The key is to stop resisting. Quiet your mind and raise your positive emotional state with mindfulness training, meditation, gratitude exercises and other proven techniques. With our combined thirty years of research into positive emotions, we know that these practices make us more creative, amplify our learning, boost our motivation and allow us to be exponentially more productive.

This is not a call to "positive thinking." Rather, it is a recommendation to use scientifically proven interventions to move you, your team and ultimately your customers from a negative and unpleasant state of emotions that maintains your focus on limiting beliefs to a positive and pleasant state of emotions that changes how you perceive yourselves, the world, and your role in it.

BUILDING A TEAM OF PROPHETS

The awareness that all humanity faces this contrast between desires and beliefs will help you navigate your transformation. Most people focus on the emotional unpleasantness that arises from the conflict within themselves between these two states. With the knowledge that these both exist in every person, you and your team can pay attention when unpleasant feelings arise within yourselves to determine what it is that you desire and what it is you believe. Your whole team can learn to communicate from this perspective which will accelerate individual and organizational transformation.

As your team becomes more aware of the contrast between desires and beliefs, they will take on one of the traits of prophets. They will be able to see the present state of these, and the future possibilities simultaneously. They will know the reality of the moment and the reality of what is possible. This will give your team the ProphetAbility to find solutions for the customer who desires to become a new person, but who has not yet taken action because they do not believe they can become that person because they are arguing in support of their limitations.

Great products, services and experiences transform customers because they help the customer believe they can take a step in the direction of becoming a version of the person who they want to become. Threats, obstacles, and risks of taking action are mitigated or eliminated. The gains of taking action plus the pains of staying where they are seem to outweigh the pains of taking action plus the gains of staying where they are.

FINAL THOUGHTS

When Tony and I first decided to write a book, we weren't exactly sure where it would go. Because we have both studied personal development and achievement for a combined thirty years, we came to the conclusion that we needed to stay open to where the road would take us. We were having our own human experience, and knew that writing this book would indeed be transformative for both of us.

Understanding at a deep level how the human experience plays into business is a concept that got us both really excited, and we couldn't wait to share our thoughts and research. We believe that understanding humans is the key to driving a successful business, as you were able to see in the stories we told. When you can really hear and understand what your customers are saying, what they are not saying, what they are feeling, aspiring to, etc., you have a unique competitive advantage that that allows you to see well into the future.

We spent a lot of time kicking around various concepts, as Tony's work focuses on the bottom-up approach to customer insights, while my work focuses on the top-down approach. We believe both are critical for companies who want to lead the inevitable disruption rather than being a casualty of it.

Let's face it. Businesses are in business to make money. Many find the "touchy feely woo woo" human experience talk a bit much to take. But hopefully after reading this book, you will see that there is a solid business case for diving deep into the human experience in order to drive your business and ultimately become ProphetAble. Because after all, isn't that the goal?

EPILOGUE

Transformation takes time and for many CEOs it can be filled with frustration. Ross Evans, the CEO of Xtracycle, related this in a conversation we had shortly before this book was released. Evans shared how after receiving the recommendations from Tony on how to improve the positioning of Xtracycle, marketing messages, and customer experiences, there were many challenges. For starters, the company had to build the B2C marketing team and the marketing engine that team would use. Then, they had to create the content that would attract customers.

"I was frustrated most by how long it took to build the team and tools to get to the vision we could plainly see. It is one thing to have the vision and another thing to realize that vision by turning it into a rough idea, then honing it, and finally creating a repeatable process that was automated."

In this statement Evans summarizes the role and the challenge for every CEO. He is accurately describing the process of harmonizing the divergent forces of the prophets and the priests. In practice, this is precisely what disrupting the status quo, tradition and culture looks like. At the same time it is the process of reestablishing a new normal, with new traditions that support the processes and culture required for success as the company becomes that which the CEO envisions.

When challenges arise in your business we encourage you to return to each of the stories for inspiration. We especially recommend that you consider the story of Maurice Herrera and Weight Watchers when you feel frustrated with the process of transformation. Recall how Herrera worked for two years before the Wall Street analysts saw signs of improvement. The story the public saw was only a portion of reality. The CEO who he started working for, Chambers, left the company weeks before the first growth in quarterly enrollments was made public. It takes great courage to be a prophet and to listen to or act on what your customers are telling you. Regardless of the challenge, you must summon the courage to hold the vision of the future while acting to create that future in the present.

The work of transformation can be hard. But, it is far more painful to settle for mediocrity and to resist human nature's call to transform. Your customers will always desire to be more, do more and have more. Invest in transforming who you are so you can lead the transformation of your company and contribute to the transformation of your team, your customers and the world.

RESOURCES AND CITATIONS

All websites were accessed between March 10 and June 14, 2018

A Chain of Innovation: The Creation of Swiffer
https://www.tandfonline.com/doi/abs/10.5437/08956308X570300
8?journalCode=urtm20

A Day in the Life Of GM CEO Mary Barra
https://www.wsj.com/articles/a-day-in-the-life-of-gm-ceo-mary-
barra-1461601044

**Americans Have Fewer Friends Outside the Family, Duke
Study Shows**
https://today.duke.edu/2006/06/socialisolation.html

Ana Live Blog, Day Two: Not Just Twerking For the Sake Of It
http://adage.com/article/special-report-ana-annual-meeting-
2017/ana-live-blog-day/310781/

Ana Masters Of Marketing Day 3 Recap
https://www.bionic-ads.com/2017/10/ana-masters-of-marketing-
day-3-recap/

Ancient Sea Rise Tale Told Accurately For 10,000 Years
https://www.scientificamerican.com/article/ancient-sea-rise-tale-
told-accurately-for-10-000-years/

Badges in Social Media: A Social Psychological Perspective
http://gamification-research.org/wp-content/uploads/2011/04/03-
Antin-Churchill.pdf

Beyond Happiness: Flourishing-PERMA Model
https://www.youtube.com/watch?v=OWavCPydQ5k&t=102s

Blink: The Power Of Thinking Without Thinking
Malcolm Gladwell - Penguin Books - 2006

Bringing Weight Watchers Back From "The Brink of Irrelevance"
http://digobrands.com/bringing-weight-watchers-back-from-the-brink-of-irrelevance/

By 2030, 95% Of Car Miles Will Be in Autonomous Shared Electric Vehicles
https://www.edmunds.com/car-news/auto-industry/by-2030-95-percent-of-car-miles-will-be-in-autonomous-shared-electric-vehicles.html

Cadillac Challenges Tesla With a Super Smart Self-driving System
https://www.wired.com/story/cadillac-super-cruise-self-driving-gm/?intcid=inline_amp

Casper Disrupted a $29 Billion Industry. Now, Its Business Model Is Getting a Complete Makeover
https://www.inc.com/cameron-albert-deitch/casper-2017-company-of-the-year-nominee.html

Chance The Rapper's Earnings Show Just How Much The Music Industry Has Changed
https://www.forbes.com/sites/hughmcintyre/2017/09/28/chance-the-rappers-earnings-show-just-how-much-the-music-industry-has-changed/#141ca4d3780f

Conceptual Consumption
http://www.people.hbs.edu/mnorton/ariely%20norton%202009.pdf

Couch To 5k: Meet The Man Who Got America Up And Running
https://blog.health.nokia.com/blog/2016/04/14/couch-to-5k-inventor-josh-clark/

Customer Disengagement
https://www.slideshare.net/WFAMarketers/customer-disengagement

Definitive Guide to Selling to Multiple Decision Makers
https://business.linkedin.com/content/dam/me/business/en-us/sales-solutions/resources/pdfs/linkedins-definitive-guide-to-selling-to-multiple-decision-makers.pdf

Delphi
https://en.wikipedia.org/wiki/Delphi

Delphi: The Oracle At Delphi
https://www.coastal.edu/intranet/ashes2art/delphi2/misc-essays/oracle_of_delphi.html

Employee Engagement in U.S. Stagnant in 2015
http://news.gallup.com/poll/188144/employee-engagement-stagnant-2015.aspx

Facebook Now Has 2 Billion Monthly Users... and Responsibility
https://techcrunch.com/2017/06/27/facebook-2-billion-users/

Flourish
Martin Seligman - Random House Australia – 2012

Food Industry Giant Nestle Unveils Big Changes
https://thebossmagazine.com/nestle-food-industry-shifts/

From Near Bankruptcy To Industry Leader: How Listening Turned Around IBM
https://www.vocoli.com/blog/june-2015/from-near-bankruptcy-to-industry-leader-how-listening-turned-around-ibm/

General Motors Is Going All Electric
https://www.wired.com/story/general-motors-electric-cars-plan-gm/

Generations Apart: New Allianz Life Study Confirms Financially Concerned Boomers, Reveals Hopeless Generation X
http://www.businesswire.com/news/home/20150506005812/en/Generations-Allianz-Life-Study-Confirms-Financially-Concerned

Gerstner: Changing Culture At IBM
https://hbswk.hbs.edu/archive/gerstner-changing-culture-at-ibm-lou-gerstner-discusses-changing-the-culture-at-ibm

GM and Cruise's Self-driving Car: Just Add Software
https://www.wired.com/story/gm-cruise-generation-3-self-driving-car/?intcid=inline_amp

GM Races To Build a Formula For Profitable Electric Cars
https://www.google.com/amp/s/mobile.reuters.com/article/amp/i dUSKBN1EY0GG

Grit: Why Passion and Resilience Are the Secrets To Success
Angela Duckworth - Vermilion – 2017

Grocery Stores Carry 40,000 More Items Than They Did in the 1990s
https://www.marketwatch.com/story/grocery-stores-carry-40000-more-items-than-they-did-in-the-1990s-2017-06-07

Hedonic Treadmill
https://en.wikipedia.org/wiki/Hedonic_treadmill

Here's How Drug Prices Actually Work
http://fortune.com/2016/04/26/drug-prices-valeant-pfizer-merck/

History of the Iroquois Indians
https://www.departments.bucknell.edu/environmental_center/sunb ury/website/HistoryofIroquoisIndians.shtml

How Casper Flipped the Mattress Industry
http://fortune.com/2017/08/23/casper-mattress-philip-krim/

How Do Your Genes Influence Levels Of Emotional Sensitivity?
https://www.psychologytoday.com/us/blog/the-athletes-way/201505/how-do-your-genes-influence-levels-emotional-sensitivity

How Employee Engagement Drives Growth
http://news.gallup.com/businessjournal/163130/employee-engagement-drives-growth.aspx

How Frustration Can Make Us More Creative
https://www.ted.com/talks/tim_harford_how_messy_problems_can_inspire_creativity

How GM Beat Tesla To the First True Mass-market Electric Car
https://www.wired.com/2016/01/gm-electric-car-chevy-bolt-mary-barra/?intcid=inline_amp

How Marketing Turned the EpiPen Into a Billion-dollar Business
http://www.bloomberg.com/news/articles/2015-09-23/how-marketing-turned-the-epipen-into-a-billion-dollar-business

How To Open Up the Next Level Of Human
https://www.youtube.com/watch?v=7xnbUT3rOvQ

Human Brain - Neuroscience - Cognitive Science
http://www.basicknowledge101.com/subjects/brain.html

IBM
https://en.wikipedia.org/wiki/IBM

Impact of Consumer Self-Image and Demographics on Preference for Healthy Labeled Food
journals.sagepub.com/doi/abs/10.1177/2158244016677325

Indra Nooyi
https://en.wikipedia.org/wiki/Indra_Nooyi

Is Your Empathy Determined by Your Genes?
https://greatergood.berkeley.edu/article/item/is_your_empathy_determined_by_your_genes

Leadership
https://www.gm.com/company/leadership/corporate-officers/mary-barra.html

London Based Coffee Carts Help The Homeless
https://www.youtube.com/watch?v=0TcNmW5UmbQ&t=47s

Lost 'epic Of Gilgamesh' Verse Depicts Cacophonous Abode Of Gods
https://www.livescience.com/52372-new-tablet-gilgamesh-epic.htm

Love 2.0: How Our Supreme Emotion Affects Everything We Think, Do, Feel, and Become
Barbara Fredrickson - Hudson Street Press – 2013

Martin Seligman Authentic Happiness Discussion
https://www.youtube.com/watch?v=Em-VqtpNrgg

Martin Seligman 'Flourishing - a New Understanding Of Wellbeing' At Happiness & Its Causes 2012
https://www.youtube.com/watch?v=e0LbwEVnfJA&t=1458s

McDonald's Is Launching a Mcvegan Burger in Sweden and Finland
http://money.cnn.com/2017/12/19/news/mcdonalds-mcvegan-vegan-burger/index.html?iid=EL

Mindset: the New Psychology Of Success
Carol Dweck - Ballantine Books - 2008

Misbehaving the Making Of Behavioral Economics
Richard Thaler - Penguin – 2016

Moral Molecule: How Trust Works
Paul Zak - Penguin Group - 2013

Most Exciting Development For Weight Watchers' Top Marketer? Oprah, Of Course!
https://marketingland.com/exciting-development-weight-watchers-top-marketer-oprah-course-190073

Mylan Price Hikes on Many Other Drugs Eclipsed Epipen Increases
http://www.statnews.com/pharmalot/2016/08/24/mylan-generic-drug-price-hikes/

Napster
https://en.wikipedia.org/wiki/Napster

Napster Shut Down
https://abcnews.go.com/Technology/story?id=119627&page=1

New Evidence Of the Geological Origins Of the Ancient Delphic Oracle (Greece)
https://www.nature.com/news/2001/010717/full/news010719-10.html

New G.M. Chief Is Company Woman, Born To It
https://mobile.nytimes.com/2013/12/11/business/gm-names-first-female-chief-executive.html

Omnipork: Vegetarian Company Wants To Disrupt China's Meat Industry
http://money.cnn.com/2018/04/23/smallbusiness/meatless-pork-china/index.html

Our Stories, Ourselves
http://www.apa.org/monitor/2011/01/stories.aspx

Pepsico Ceo Indra Nooyi's Desire To Create Snacks For Women Is Nothing New
http://fortune.com/2018/02/05/doritos-pepsico-indra-nooyi/

Pepsico Ceo Indra Nooyi's Long-term Strategy Put Her Job in Jeopardy - but Now the Numbers Are In, and the Analysts Who Doubted Her Will Have To Eat Their Words
http://www.businessinsider.fr/us/indra-nooyi-pepsico-push-for-long-term-value-2018-1

Pepsico's Ceo Was Right. Now What?
http://fortune.com/2015/06/05/pepsico-ceo-indra-nooyi/

PERMA
https://www.youtube.com/watch?v=iK6K_N2qe9Y

Pixar Storytelling Rules #5: Essence Of Structure
https://www.youtube.com/watch?v=C7D8yDB7Tlk

Pixar: The Story Behind the Studio
https://www.youtube.com/watch?v=MSkeNmz7v4M

Positivity: Groundbreaking Research To Release Your Inner Optimist and Thrive
Barbara Fredrickson - Oneworld - 2011

'Power Women' Member Nooyi To Lead 'platinum' Pepsi
https://www.forbes.com/2006/08/14/pepsi-nooyi-ceo-cx_gl_0814autofacescan10.html

Procter & Gamble: Swiffer
https://www.continuuminnovation.com/en/what-we-do/case-studies/swiffer/

Report: Employee Engagement Benchmark Study, 2016
https://experiencematters.blog/2016/02/16/report-employee-engagement-benchmark-study-2016/

Selling Pain to the Saturated Self
https://orca.cf.ac.uk/96293/3/TM%25201910%5B1%5D.pdf

Shooting the Messenger
https://en.wikipedia.org/wiki/Shooting_the_messenger

Six Stats on the Importance Of Trust in Influencer Marketing
https://searchenginewatch.com/2017/02/21/six-stats-on-the-importance-of-trust-in-influencer-marketing/

Stealing Fire: How Silicon Valley, the Navy Seals, and Maverick Scientists Are Revolutionizing the Way We Live and Work
Steven Kotler-Jamie Wheal - Dey St., an Imprint Of William Morrow - 2017

Taylor Swift Takes a Stand Over Spotify Music Royalties
https://www.theguardian.com/music/2014/nov/04/taylor-swift-spotify-streaming-album-sales-snub

The B2B Elements Of Value
https://hbr.org/2018/03/the-b2b-elements-of-value

The Chevy Bolt Is Crushing the Tesla Model 3
http://www.businessinsider.com/chevy-bolt-crushing-tesla-model-3-2018-1

The Demise of Toys 'R' Us Is a Warning
https://www.theatlantic.com/magazine/archive/2018/07/toys-r-us-bankruptcy-private-equity/561758/

The Development of Purpose During Adolescence
https://web.stanford.edu/group/adolescence/cgi-bin/coa/sites/default/files/devofpurpose_0.pdf

The Emotional Combinations That Make Stories Go Viral
https://hbr.org/2016/05/research-the-link-between-feeling-in-control-and-viral-content

The Experience Economy Updated Edition
Pine Joseph-James Gilmore - Harvard Business Review - 2011

The Happy Secret To Better Work
https://www.ted.com/talks/shawn_achor_the_happy_secret_to_better_work

The Hope Circuit - Dr. Martin Seligman
https://www.youtube.com/watch?v=F8I-F3LZ2ZA&t=4135s

The Ideal Praise-to-criticism Ratio
https://hbr.org/2013/03/the-ideal-praise-to-criticism

The Influence of In-Store Music on Wine Selections
https://www.researchgate.net/publication/232593421_The_Influence_of_In-Store_Music_on_Wine_Selections

The Magic Relationship Ratio, According To Science
https://www.gottman.com/blog/the-magic-relationship-ratio-according-science/

The Narrative Reconstruction Of Psychotherapy and Psychological Health
https://www.tandfonline.com/doi/abs/10.1080/10503300802326020

The Nature of Awe: Elicitors, Appraisals, and Effects on Self-Concept
https://greatergood.berkeley.edu/dacherkeltner/docs/shiota.2007.pdf

The Power Of Meaning: Finding Fulfillment in a World Obsessed with Happiness
Emily Smith - Broadway Books - 2017

The Science Of Storytelling: Why Telling a Story Is the Most Powerful Way To Activate Our Brains
https://lifehacker.com/5965703/the-science-of-storytelling-why-telling-a-story-is-the-most-powerful-way-to-activate-our-brains

The Self-Concept in Buyer Behavior
https://www.sciencedirect.com/science/article/pii/0007681377900593

The Undoing Project: a Friendship That Changed Our Minds
Michael Lewis - W.W. Norton & Company - 2017

The 30 Elements Of Consumer Value: A Hierarchy
https://hbr.org/2016/09/the-elements-of-value

To Sell Is Human: the Surprising Truth About Persuading, Convincing, and Influencing Others
DANIEL PINK - Canongate Books Ltd - 2018

Topic: Starbucks
https://www.statista.com/topics/1246/starbucks/

Toys R Us Blames Amazon, Target, Walmart For Death Blow
https://www.usatoday.com/story/money/2018/03/15/toys-r-us-liquidation-amazon-target-walmart/427209002/

Toys R Us - How Bad Assumptions Fed Bad Financial Planning Creating Failure
https://www.forbes.com/sites/adamhartung/2017/09/20/toys-r-us-is-a-lesson-in-how-bad-assumptions-feed-bad-financial-planning-creating-failure/#20ffa1ea58ea

Updated Thinking on Positivity Ratios
www.unc.edu/peplab/publications/Fredrickson 2013 Updated Thinking.pdf

U.S. Paid Music Subscribers 2017
https://www.statista.com/statistics/707103/paid-streaming-music-subscribers-usa/

Waymo Orders 62,000 Chrysler Pacificas As Fiat Chrysler in Talks on Selling Self-driving Cars
https://electrek.co/2018/05/31/waymo-expands-chrysler-pacifica-fleet-sell-cars/

Weight Watchers Advertises During The Super Bowl For The First Time Ever; Launches "lose 10 Lbs On Us" Offer
https://www.weightwatchers.com/us/weight-watchers-advertises-during-super-bowl-first-time-ever

Weight Watchers Ceo Resigns As Oprah Winfrey's $1 Billion Golden Touch Is Gone
https://www.forbes.com/sites/nathanvardi/2016/09/12/weight-watchers-ceo-resigns-as-oprah-winfreys-1-billion-golden-touch-is-gone/#6a8189bf6f4f

Weight Watchers Goes on Ad Blitz with Oprah Spots
http://www.crainsnewyork.com/article/20161227/PROFESSIONAL_SERVICES/161229943/oprah-loses-40-pounds-and-goes-on-an-ad-blitz-with-weight-watchers

Weight Watchers Has Finally Found Its New Agency Partner in Havas
https://www.adweek.com/brand-marketing/weight-watchers-has-finally-found-its-new-agency-partner-havas-167557/

Weight Watchers Hires Marketing Vp As It Repositions Brand
http://adage.com/article/cmo-strategy/weight-watchers-hires-marketing-vp-repositions-brand/295335/

Weight Watchers Names Maurice Herrera Senior Vice President Of Marketing
https://www.prnewswire.com/news-releases/weight-watchers-names-maurice-herrera-senior-vice-president-of-marketing-278644031.html

Weight Watchers, Oprah Go 'Holistic'
https://www.foxbusiness.com/features/weight-watchers-oprah-go-holistic

Weight Watchers Seeks a New Lead Agency
https://www.adweek.com/brand-marketing/weight-watchers-seeks-new-lead-agency-163623/

Weight Watchers Ups Stacie Sherer To Corporate Comms SVP
https://www.prweek.com/article/1442899/weight-watchers-ups-stacie-sherer-corporate-comms-svp

What Makes You Happy?
https://www.youtube.com/watch?v=As-g_dwgJig

When You're Innovating, Resist Looking For Solutions
https://hbr.org/2013/09/when-youre-innovating-resist-l

Who Says Elephants Can't Dance?: Leading a Great Enterprise Through Dramatic Change
Louis Gerstner - Harperbusiness - 2004

Why Casper Is The $750 Million Startup That Just Can't Rest
https://www.fastcompany.com/40438355/why-casper-is-the-750-million-startup-that-just-cant-rest

Why Chance the Rapper Makes Music For Free (and How He Actually Makes Money)
https://www.vanityfair.com/hollywood/2017/02/why-chance-the-rapper-music-is-free-and-how-he-makes-money

Why Every Leader Should Understand Narrative Psychology
https://www.psychologytoday.com/us/blog/resilient-leadership/201607/why-every-leader-should-understand-narrative-psychology

Why Inspiring Stories Make Us React: The Neuroscience of Narrative
https://www.ncbi.nlm.nih.gov/pmc/articles/PMC4445577/

Why The Casper Business Model Makes So Much Sense
https://www.mattressclarity.com/reviews/casper/business-model/

Wieden + Kennedy Lands Weight Watchers
https://www.adweek.com/brand-marketing/wieden-kennedy-lands-weight-watchers-157111/

2016 Content Preferences Survey: B2B Buyers Value Content That Offers Data And Analysis
https://www.demandgenreport.com/resources/research/2016-content-preferences-survey-b2b-buyers-value-content-that-offers-data-and-analysis

5 Reasons Toys R Us Failed To Survive Bankruptcy
https://www.usatoday.com/story/money/2018/03/18/toys-r-us-bankruptcy-liquidation/436176002/

#wellactually, Americans Say Customer Service Is Better Than Ever
http://about.americanexpress.com/news/pr/2017/wellactually-americans-say-customer-service-better-than-ever.aspx

ProphetAbility

ABOUT THE AUTHORS

Betsy loves business.

Throughout her career, Betsy has had the privilege of observing business at the highest levels while delivering executive-level Customer Advisory Boards for companies including Dell, LexisNexis, Springer, VeriSign, and other large tech companies in the US, the Middle East, Europe and Latin America.

In addition to being an author and speaker, Betsy is an entrepreneur who understands the joys and challenges of growing a business and ensuring that the customers are served at levels that blow past expectations. What Betsy loves most about her work is knowing that every single time a group of executives gather in a boardroom for a Customer Advisory Board, there will be an aha moment that results in game-changing insights for the people around the table and for the organization at large. Every single time.

Living in Dayton, Ohio, with her husband Paul, Betsy enjoys being on the lake and spending time with their adult kids and five grandkids.

ABOUT THE AUTHORS

Tony Bodoh is constantly seeking to understand the nuances of human experience that separate the high performers from everyone else. His discoveries have led him to publish three #1 bestselling books and to found or co-found five companies ranging from customer experience consulting to television production.

Tony built the customer experience programs for some of the world's most respected companies including Gaylord Hotels. He is recognized as a thought leader in the customer service sector and was recently named #5 on the Top 16 Customer Service Movers and Shakers to follow.

Tony is an international speaker at personal growth seminars, as well as, business, analytical and technology conferences. Tony is an award-winning coach certified by both the Life Mastery Institute and Extreme Focus.

Tony resides in Nashville and is married to an amazing executive chef. He has two wonderful daughters who both earned two Guinness Book World Records before the age of 10.

HOW TO REACH BETSY AND TONY

Betsy Westhafer
The Congruity Group
Betsy@TheCongruityGroup.com
www.TheCongruityGroup.com

Tony Bodoh
Tony Bodoh International, LLC
Tony@TonyBodoh.com
www.TonyBodoh.com

MASTERMINDS AND RETREATS

To stay engaged with Tony and Betsy, join one of their
ProphetAbility mastermind groups or attend an upcoming
retreat. More details can be found at
www.ProphetAbilityBook.com.

To be alerted to upcoming events,
be sure to join the mailing list.

CREDITS

Cover design and illustrations by Victoria Ballweg Designs
Tony Bodoh's photo by Palimor Studios
Betsy Westhafer's photo by Samir Janjua
Layout and proofreading by Mitch Tomlin, The Congruity Group

ProphetAbility

47389629R00161

Made in the USA
Middletown, DE
10 June 2019